Horizon

SUMMER, 1976 • VOLUME XVIII, NUMBER 3

cHorizon

SUMMER, 1976 • VOLUME XVIII, NUMBER 3

HORIZON is published six times a year by American Heritage Publishing Co., Inc. Editorial and executive offices: 1221 Avenue of the Americas, New York, N.Y. 10020. Treasurer and Secretary: Anthony J. Sansiveri. All correspondence about subscriptions should be addressed to: HORIZON Subscription Office, 381 West Center St., Marion, Ohio 43302.

Single copies: $5.00. Subscriptions: $26.00 per year in the U.S.; Canada and elsewhere: $28.00.
Hard cover edition: Single copies: $7.50. Subscriptions: $32.00 per year in the U.S.; Canada and elsewhere: $34.00.

Cumulative indexes for Volumes I–V, VI–X, and XI–XV are available at $7.50. HORIZON is also indexed in the *Readers' Guide to Periodical Literature*. The editors welcome contributions but can assume no responsibility for unsolicited material. Title registered U.S. Patent Office. Second-class postage paid at New York, N.Y., and at additional mailing offices.

Letters

This magazine has never published letters from its readers. Why? Certainly not for lack of them. The Winter and Spring issues have provoked a number of communiqués, and since, at the moment, we have no regular place to put them, we decided to forgo the editorial for once and let our readers speak.

Kenneth Lamott's "On Controlling Human Behavior" in the Winter issue brings the following dissent:

"Anyone who thinks [as does Mr. Lamott] that Chairman Mao is the ultimate behaviorist simply does not understand the problem. The Chinese Revolution is mainly a rational and, if you will, democratic solution to one of the most stupendous economic problems of all time."

—H. W. Cone, Sacramento, California

(To whom we mildly reply that Mr. Lamott nowhere accused Chairman Mao of irrationality; he emphasized that all governments use behavior modification techniques.)

We have received this useful reminder about King James I ("The First King of Great Britain," by John Kenyon, Spring, 1976):

"I was amazed that you could devote an entire article to James I without mentioning what every American schoolchild knows, or ought to know; namely, that it was during the reign of wicked, intolerant King James that the Pilgrim fathers fled England, eventually making their way to Plymouth Rock.

"Since a large part of the same issue of HORIZON is taken up with articles about health fads, I was also surprised that you failed to say that James was opposed to smoking and in 1604 published a document that today's antismoking groups ought to revive—his famous *Counterblaste to Tobacco*."

—Katharine P. Alexander, New York, N.Y.

As to "The War that Broke the Imperial Spirit" (Spring, 1976), it had resonating effects:

"Jan Morris's account of the Boer War reminded me time and again of the American experience in Vietnam. The American failure to obtain a quick victory echoes the frustrating and costly campaign of the British against the Boer guerrillas. And 'love-it-or-leave-it' types who beat up war resisters in the sixties find their counterparts in the toughs who broke up protest meetings against the Boer War."

—Deborah N. Collins, Cleveland, Ohio

Charles L. Mee, Jr.'s review of *The Last European War* has stirred up some opposition:

"Mr. Mee puts forth the fact that the German economy was remarkably sound during the first few years of the war as a means of discrediting economic determinism. And yet he says that Germany had lost the war after December of 1941. Why?

"In fact there were very real economic reasons for the disintegration of the German war machine, and they came into play early. Long before the Wehrmacht crossed the Russian border, the Soviets were producing the finest tanks in the world simply because they had the resources to do it. Granted, the German war against Russia began in a mutual welter of stupid mistakes and lost opportunities. Nevertheless, as the war ground on, economic factors began to assert their logic. The fact remains that Russia churned out materiel faster than Germany, and in the end brought Germany down.

"And another thing. Mr. Mee tells us that America's part in the war was 'absolutely unnecessary and irrelevant.' I don't think so. Our intervention might not have been crucial but it hastened the victory by many years. In this sour post-Vietnam era, we should be proud that our country once cast its lot vigorously and effectively on the right side."

—Hiram Streeter, Quincy, Illinois

Concerning the Morris and the Mee pieces, both of which directly raise the question of whether wars are worth fighting, we have a suggestion (from Ralph Cummings of Los Alamitos, California) that both articles should be required reading for all political candidates in 1976.

Any bona fide political candidates, from Republican to Democrat to Vegetarian, are urged to apply for free copies of these articles. All other readers are invited to send comments, opinions, questions, and addenda, a selection of which will regularly appear in a Letters section in forthcoming issues. —THE EDITORS

PRIVATE COLLECTION

COVER: When Henri Matisse painted *The Pink Blouse* in 1924, he was a successfully established artist living in comfort in Nice. Some twenty years earlier, at another Mediterranean seaport, he had had to struggle to shape his own distinctive style. How he did it, and how he shocked the Parisian art world when he exhibited his brilliantly colored works, are told by John Russell in an article beginning on page 4.

HARBOR AT COLLIOURE, *lithograph, circa 1906*

The Birth of a Wild Beast

One summer early in this century
Henri Matisse took his family to the seashore.
There, in the light of the
Mediterranean, a new way of painting came forth

By JOHN RUSSELL

From his villa, through the window below, Matisse could see the harbor where boats sailed briskly (above) or bobbed at their moorings (at left). The intense light and vivid color that Matisse found at Collioure invigorated his art long after his sojourns there had ended. At right, he works on a still life in his winter studio at Issy-les-Moulineaux; in the background is his *Dance* of 1909 (see page 13), which was inspired by the fishermen he saw dancing on the beach in 1905.

THE OPEN WINDOW, *1905*

LUXE, CALME ET VOLUPTÉ—STUDY, *1904*

Matisse had spent the summer of 1904 at Saint-Tropez, where he painted this study of languorous nudes picnicking on the beach. He was tentatively beginning to use the bold hues—pinks and yellows in the sky, reds and oranges on the ground, blues and lavenders outlining the figures—that burst forth a year later in his work at Collioure. There, one peaceful day, Matisse made the sketch below of a fisherman on the rocks. In the background, a tiny figure swimming in the sea, is Matisse's companion at Collioure, the young artist André Derain.

THE FISHERMAN, *1905*

P icasso was the one who suggested that Henri Matisse and his family spend the summer of 1905 at Collioure. Matisse's son Pierre had been ailing. The nineteenth-century belief that "a change of air" can cure anything was still current. Picasso said, "Try Collioure," and off they went. (Mme Matisse had had a look at the place beforehand and thought it seemed all right.)

Collioure already had a good name among painters. Paul Signac had been there in 1887 and had painted the old fortress overlooking the bay so that it looked as big as Alcatraz and twice as impregnable. Collioure was a pleasant little town where living was very cheap and the air was pure, even by the standards of the day. It was on the Mediterranean coast, no more than a mile or two from Spain, and life there had certain echoes of Spanish ways: above all the round dance, the *sardana*, which was danced on the beach to the accompaniment of an ad hoc wind band.

Three Mediterranean villages were to play a great part in the art of the twentieth century. Céret, a town in the hills not far from Collioure, was one of them; there Pablo Picasso and Georges Braque spent summers at a crucial period in the development of cubism. Another was Cadaqués, a little fishing village just across the Spanish border where in 1908 Picasso painted some of the toughest and densest and most difficult of all his paintings. The third was Collioure. For Henri Matisse, for André Derain (Matisse's companion that summer of 1905), and later for Juan Gris, it was a place where something very important happened.

They were none of them places of sensational beauty. All that they had in common was that they were a long way from Paris, demanded a minimum of social contacts, had an uncontaminated local life, and cost almost nothing. They lay in countrysides that were quite undeveloped and they kept to a style of life that was plain, dignified, and unpretentious. The same could be said even of Saint-Tropez at that time, but there was something about the isolation of the three Cs—Collioure, Céret, Cadaqués—that was particularly propitious for uninterrupted work. There is work that can be done best in big cities, and there is work that calls for a long privacy; for Henri Matisse, winter in Paris and summer in Collioure was to prove as good a formula as could be found.

Matisse was in his middle thirties. As an artist, he had been a late beginner and was still a slow developer. In 1905 few people would have picked him out as a man destined to be one of the greatest of all European artists. Yet today that is how we see him: as painter, as draftsman, as sculptor, and as the creator in his late seventies of a completely new medium—colored paper cutouts—that allowed him to carve color as a sculptor carves marble.* In 1905 little of this innovative mastery had emerged; to his younger colleagues Matisse seemed to be prematurely aged, like a provincial savant long set in his ways, from whom nothing astonishing could be expected.

He had plenty to look serious about. By birth and by temperament he was a worrier, a man from the burdened north. Reared in a conspicuously hideous countryside (between Arras and Sedan, in northern France), he had no idea that Nature could be essentially voluptuous. Nature as provider was one thing; even between Arras and Sedan she could be relied upon for turnips and potatoes. But Nature as playmate? Nature as seductress? Nature as a metaphor for opulence and fecundity? No such idea had presented itself to the square-built, strong-jawed young student who went to Paris in 1887 to study law. Why he had opted for law nobody knew, perhaps least of all himself. He was a quiet,

*See "Matisse's Final Flowering," HORIZON, Winter, 1970.

VIEW OF COLLIOURE, *by André Derain, 1905*

Near the Spanish border on the Mediterranean Golfe du Lion, Collioure, at left, is a busy fishing port guarded by rugged fortifications. In Derain's lively painting of the harbor, above, fishermen dry their nets on the quay, while behind them their boats lie at anchor. In a letter to his friend Maurice de Vlaminck, Derain wrote that his trip to Collioure in 1905 had taught him "a new conception of light, which is as follows: a complete negation of shadow. Here the light is very strong, shadows are very thin. . . . It is a world of reflections."

André Derain, by Maurice de Vlaminck

PORTRAIT OF MME MATISSE, *1905*

After they returned to Paris in 1905, Matisse painted this famous portrait of his wife, Amélie. One dismayed critic wrote of it: "Alas! when he paints his wife with a broad stripe of green down her nose, though it startlingly suggests her, it is punishment to have made her appear so to you always." Back at Collioure the following summer, Matisse painted his own face (below) as if it were a rough landscape—all greens and browns —and also did a striking picture of a sailor, opposite.

SELF-PORTRAIT, *1906*

steady, inconspicuous young man with nothing much to say and no clearly defined bent. If he were a "great artist" in a novel or a film, he would be presented to us at that stage in his life as on fire for art. He would be shown responding to the great men who were, in fact, that very year shaping the future of art: Georges Seurat, Paul Cézanne, Vincent van Gogh, Paul Gauguin. The novelist or film director might not bend history to the point of having Matisse on terms of personal acquaintance with any of them, but it would certainly seem implausible to a creator of fiction that Matisse at the age of eighteen would care nothing for painting, good or bad.

Yet that is how it was. It was as if he was anesthetized where art was concerned. He read his law books, and he passed his examinations, and he went back to the sodden north, and he got a little job in a law firm, and he pushed his pen for the prescribed number of hours every day, and that was all. He does not seem to have had any sense of his identity as an independent human being; to himself, and probably to others, he seemed blank, torpid, purposeless, unawakened.

But then, in 1890, when he was nearly twenty-one, Henri Matisse got sick. His appendix had to be removed. Recovery was unexpectedly slow, and he lay in bed with time on his hands. At some point in his long and tedious convalescence his mother gave him a Sunday painter's box of paints, a set of brushes, and an instruction book. Matisse opened the book, took up the brushes, and set to work copying a landscape, one of the chromolithographs that were the debased currency of art at the time. The effect on Matisse was miraculous. "For the first time in my life," he said later, "I felt free, quiet, and on my own."

It is important to remember, in this context, that Matisse talked and wrote sparingly and was the most prosaic of men. He never wasted a word or exaggerated a feeling. So we can believe what he said some sixty years later, remembering how he felt when he first took the brushes in his hand: "It was as if I had been called. Thereafter, I did not lead my life. It led me." To begin with, it led him to art school. To a life of unremitting labor: ten, twelve, fourteen hours a day, every day for sixty years. To a way of life remarkable, above all, for its self-sufficiency and for the corollary of that self-sufficiency, an absolute inner loneliness. Matisse sacrificed everything for his work. His wife, his children, his friends: all came second. "Never waste time!" was his favorite maxim. "Persevere!" was another. Great art exacts its price, and in the case of Henri Matisse human contacts ranked low; he felt they were a waste of time and an impediment to perseverance.

Thus described, he doesn't sound like the ideal summer companion. Even in later years, when his mastership was no longer in doubt, he worked in a state of high nervous tension. In 1905 "Truth at any cost" was already his motto, but he did not know quite what "truth" was, and still less did he know how to get through to it. In fifteen years of hard, slow work he had sometimes glimpsed his own true way, only to lose sight of it again. Sometimes he had been affected by others, most notably his early teacher at the Ecole des Beaux-Arts, Gustave Moreau, and later Cézanne, whose work he knew from visits to the art dealer Ambroise Vollard. Sometimes he had bogged down (it seemed at the time) in obsessional studies that bore no immediate fruit. In Paris he was all over town, day after day, chasing from one schoolroom to another, painting, drawing, sculpting. The summer was, or should have been, the time to decide what direction his art should take.

THE YOUNG SAILOR, II, *1906*

MARGUERITE READING, *1906*

Marguerite, the eldest of the three Matisse children, sits in the villa at Collioure, absorbed in her summer reading. Posing frequently and patiently for her father, she figures in several other early works, including the drawing below, in which she holds a sleepy cat.

GIRL WITH BLACK CAT, *1910*

It was vital that he do so. In 1898 he had married a beautiful young woman, Amélie-Noélie-Alexandrine Parayre, and now they had three children to look after. He had very little money, and yet it was not in Matisse's nature either to hurry or to compromise. He had spent the previous summer in Saint-Tropez with Paul Signac and a group of Signac's friends. They had been kind to him, but he didn't get from them what he needed: the to-and-fro of independent exchange among equals. Signac was too much the older master, and Matisse was not willing to go cap in hand to someone whose accomplishments, though real, were not the ones he could best profit by. ("Who wants to live with a lot of provincial aunts?" he said of Signac's followers.)

The summer of 1905 was different. In André Derain he had a friend and colleague ten years younger than himself who was in many ways his exact opposite. Where Matisse was anxious, concentrated, prudent, slow to move, quietly dressed, and in outward things the very model of middle-class morality, Derain was an outgoing giant who didn't care what he did or what he looked like or what was thought of him. The son of a prosperous dairyman, Derain behaved as if the word "inhibition" was not in the dictionary. In the winter he was as likely to camp out in an abandoned restaurant, burning furniture to keep warm, as to come home in the evening. In the summer he roamed the countryside in piratical style, bicycling as much as a hundred miles a day, rowing in regattas if he felt like it, playing practical jokes, and making love to every girl he could get his hands on.

Yet this same André Derain was a devoted student of the old masters and had made perfectly good copies of paintings in the Louvre while he was still in his teens. He had read widely and discerningly in physics at a time when the existing notion of the universe was being sent to the junk yard and a completely new one was being born. He had ideas of his own about philosophy, about the theatre, about the rights and wrongs of colonial government, and—most of all, perhaps—about the future of painting. He was a champion verbalizer, a nonstop ruminator, arguer, commentator, and prophet, and in this, too, he was the opposite of Matisse. Where Matisse waited to get one thought exactly right before starting on another, Derain would grasshopper this way and that, mingling sense and nonsense, sober truth and provocation, outrage and divination. Thinking of them that summer, we may well imagine that, like Don Quixote and Sancho Panza, Don Juan and Leporello, Hamlet and Horatio, they complemented one another to perfection.

Derain had committed himself on the future of art as early as 1901, two years after he had first met Matisse. "As for painting," he wrote to a friend, "I realize that the period of realism is over. Where painting is concerned, we're only beginning." By "realism" he meant the imitation of nature. In his view painting should offer not an imitation of nature but an equivalent of it. Writing at a time when impressionism was still abhorrent to most French people, Derain had already dismissed the impressionists for trying to copy nature: "The great mistake that painters have made is to attempt to render the fugitive effects of nature. It has never struck them that what makes those effects so arresting has nothing to do with what makes a good painting." Matisse was to express much the same thought in 1908: "A rapid rendering of a landscape represents only one moment of its existence. I prefer, by insisting upon its essential character, to risk losing charm in order to obtain greater stability."

Imitation of the kind Derain and Matisse decried gives us at best a

SIESTA, OR INTERIOR AT COLLIOURE, *1905*

MME MATISSE AMONG THE OLIVE TREES, *1905*

Even on the hottest days, Matisse worked as long as fourteen hours—sketching, painting, sculpting, indoors and out. But, like any vacationing family, the Matisses found time for naps and for walks in the countryside. While Mme Matisse rests in the bedroom, above, Marguerite stands on the balcony and gazes out at the sea. Matisse had a difficult time getting his two boys to pose for him, but little Pierre did sit still long enough for his father to model the smiling portrait head below.

CHILD'S HEAD, *1905*

THE BLUE NUDE (SOUVENIR OF BISKRA), *1907*

Only because of a mishap did Matisse paint the robust odalisque above. One day at Collioure, while sculpting a reclining nude, he knocked the clay model from its stand. Exasperated, he decided not to repair the damage right away, but to paint a similarly posed nude instead. Behind her, in the background, he placed palm leaves like some he had seen on a trip the year before to Biskra in Algeria. Her forceful angularity is even more pronounced in the finally completed sculpture below.

RECLINING NUDE, I, *1907*

low-keyed satisfaction. It confirms us in our own everyday vision, but it cannot give us that sense of heightened vitality, or life quickened and intensified, that great painting has to offer. André Derain was anything but low-keyed, and he knew enough of art history to realize that the next step would involve color. As Vincent van Gogh had written, "The future of art lies with a colorist such as there has never been before." And what had Paul Gauguin said? That "a pound of green is more green than an ounce of green." "Color for color's sake!" was Derain's succinct way of putting it.

The primacy of color was not invented by either Matisse or Derain. It had been stated by Paul Gauguin, both by his own example and in conversations in Brittany with the young painters who admired him. It was being explored by others in France, and it was also being mooted by Ernst Ludwig Kirchner and his friends in Dresden, and by Wassily Kandinsky, first in Russia and later in Munich. It was in the air, irresistibly. But it had to be brought down to earth, and that is what happened in Matisse's and Derain's paintings at Collioure.

There is always room in history for what people call "accident," and thus it was that Matisse and Derain were taken, while at Collioure, to see the painter Daniel de Monfreid. Monfreid had been a close friend of Gauguin's during Gauguin's years in France, and he had several of Gauguin's South Seas paintings on his walls. Matisse needed no persuading where Gauguin was concerned, and in fact he had once bought a *Head of a Boy* by Gauguin at a time when he had little money to spare. But it was with Gauguin as it was with most of Matisse's admirations: he did not rush to emulate, but kept Gauguin in mind until the moment was right. In the summer of 1905 the moment *was* right, and Matisse followed Gauguin's instructions, which were in effect that "color is not as it is. It is what you want it to be." As Paul Signac had said: "The triumphant colorist has only to appear. We have prepared his palette for him."

The palette wasn't everything, of course. No matter how lucid or how dexterous its arrangement, it still had to be keyed to a specific subject. The colors had to make sense in terms of the painting's subject matter, not just in terms of theory. Signac's own paintings in the 1880's had ended up looking both bland and cautious; in later life they became loud and lacked subtlety. Signac knew how to write about color, but he never learned how to use it. The unit of statement to which he and his friends held fast was the dot, and the dot by its very nature resulted in a speckly, in-between-colors effect. Matisse and Derain were never dot men. They were brush men, delighting in the movement of the laden brush across the canvas. For nothing in the world would they have given up that fundamental sensation. Matisse tussled with the dot for as long as he could bear it, and he even went on tussling with it in Collioure. But it finally seemed to him that one color neutralized another when the dots were placed next to each other. It was a happy day for him when he abandoned the dot altogether and began to apply his colors one by one with thick, well-nourished strokes.

After Matisse and Derain returned to Paris, some of the pictures they painted at Collioure were shown at the Salon d'Automne. One ill-tempered critic wrote, "What is presented to us here—apart from the materials employed—has nothing whatever to do with painting: some formless confusion of colors; blue, red, yellow, green; some splotches of pigment crudely juxtaposed; the barbaric and naive sport of a child who plays with the box of colors he just got as a Christmas present." Another critic, Louis Vauxcelles, achieved fame in art history by calling the new paintings the works of "wild beasts" (*fauves* in French). The term "Fauve" is still in use, though no one was ever less of a wild beast than Henri Matisse, and the paintings themselves do not seem to most of us to have an animal quality at all. They stand, rather, for an aesthetic of pure exhilaration. Elsewhere and at other times the emancipation of color had all manner of overtones: social, economic, mystical. In Germany, in the work of Ernst Kirchner and Emil Nolde, it was by implication an attack on a hypocritical and militaristic society. In Norway it stood for the sensations of horror and dread that overcame one man, Edvard Munch. In Russia it was linked to the discovery of peasant arts by artists like Kandinsky. In the case of Kandinsky it was connected with the hope of a more truly spiritual society. But none of these considerations entered into the experiments of Matisse and Derain. They just painted that way because they wanted to and because they felt that it was the right direction for painting to go. Derain felt that Fauve painting was historically determined; Matisse felt that it was right for Matisse, and that what was right for Matisse would turn out to be right for painting in general. From the one belief, as from the other, there flowed an exceptional assurance that still communicates itself to us whenever we see the paintings in question.

Although Matisse and Derain complemented one another, it turned out during their time in Collioure that their respective roles were reversible rather than fixed once and for all. Sometimes it was Derain who felt anxious and uncertain, only to be lifted back onto the rails by Matisse; when Matisse was in crisis, Derain showed unexpected reserves of quiet and logical reasoning. And in the evenings, when Derain settled in for a long, serious talk about painting, Matisse surprised him by his capacity

TWO SKETCHES OF A NUDE GIRL PLAYING A FLUTE, *1905–1906*

Matisse returned again and again to the subject of nude figures disporting themselves outdoors, a well-loved theme in the history of Western painting. The young girl fingering her flute above is a study for *Joy of Life*, completed in 1906, a large composition of figures in an Arcadian landscape. In 1909 he painted one of several versions of nude dancers, below. The hands of the two figures in the foreground—reaching, yet not quite touching—emphasize the tugging tension of the circle.

DANCE, *1909*

LE LUXE, I, *1907*

Although painted at Collioure, *Le Luxe, I,* above, is a dream world inhabited by self-absorbed, untroubled goddesses. The shoreline and the hills behind them echo their simplified, rounded forms; all is calm and harmonious. "Expression for me," Matisse wrote in 1908, "does not reside in passions glowing in a human face or manifested by violent movement. The entire arrangement of my picture is expressive." In its deep greens and browns, the view of Collioure and the sea, opposite, expresses the feeling of a cool, shady grove on a summer afternoon.

for abstract speculation. Altogether, theirs was one of those marriages of minds that have been so valuable to the art of our century.

Collioure is still much as it was in 1905; unlike Saint-Tropez, it has kept its original character and is still a discreet little town way off the tourist routes. The stern line of its fortifications, the massive jut of the fortress, the lighthouse, the brightly painted boats drawn up on the beach, the color-washed houses, the trees whose branches seem to fold into one another—all are still there. The range of color is still intense, the grand setting of sea and sky unaltered. Even the *sardana* is still danced on the beach, with the ad hoc orchestra still squeaking its way through the same two or three tunes. Nature came halfway to meet Matisse and Derain; it's all there, but someone had to see that landscape for the first time as it really is and to go on from there to re-create it with a heightened palette.

That is what Matisse and Derain did. When they painted a row of tree trunks, they did not make them a uniform and cautious brown. They made them scarlet, purple, dark green, violet, maroon, ultramarine, yellow-green. The earth was orange, blue, pale green, ocher. The trees had lavender leaves, vermilion leaves, leaves the color of a fresh green almond. In Matisse's *Open Window* (page 4) and in Derain's *View of Collioure* (page 7) the colors do not merge, but bounce off one another with a cumulative effect that is irresistibly festive. These must be some of the happiest pictures ever painted. They were not, by the way, what people call "orgies of color." Everything in them held together. Matisse never chose his colors at random; when he showed one of his paintings to the aged Renoir, Renoir looked at it long and hard and said afterward, "I thought he just waved the brush about, but not at all! He couldn't have taken more trouble."

In his *Notes of a Painter*, which he wrote in 1908, Matisse describes his careful placement of color on the canvas: "Suppose I have to paint an interior: I have before me a cupboard; it gives me a sensation of vivid red, and I put down a red that satisfies me. A relation is established between this red and the white of the canvas. Let me put a green near the red, and make the floor yellow; and again there will be relationships between the green or yellow and the white of the canvas which will satisfy me. But these different tones mutually weaken one another. . . . I cannot copy nature in a servile way; I am forced to interpret nature and submit it to the spirit of the picture."

Landscape and still life were one thing, the human face quite another. People will accept the reinvention of trees or cupboards, and yet cry out in horror at the reinvention of the human form. Something of atavistic fear is added to the element of aesthetic exasperation when faces are tampered with. Yet nothing of the sort deterred Matisse or Derain when they painted each other at Collioure in 1905, and the two little paintings now seem to us to be vivid and penetrating portraits, as do the two portraits of Mme Matisse that Matisse painted in what might be called "Collioure style" when they got back to Paris. One came to be known as the "Green Line" (page 8), after the color of the shadow on Mme Matisse's nose. In the other, *The Green Hat*, Mme Matisse wears a large, fashionable bonnet that had a special meaning for both painter and sitter: Mme Matisse supplemented the family income in hard times by moonlighting as a milliner. At a distance of seventy years we can distinguish between the ostentatious finery of Mme Matisse's costume and the sensitive and vulnerable quality of the face that looks out at us. But

VIEW OF COLLIOURE, *1908*

in 1905 the whole venture seemed outlandish and unacceptable. People would not believe that a green hat could cast a green shadow on the wearer's brow, or that the nose in its turn could cast a green shadow on cheeks streaked with pink and red. The colors of Collioure, from Naples yellow to bright orange and from vermilion to violet, were all there in this portrait. And Matisse got them to live together in ways which now seem to us perfectly and completely resolved.

Matisse did not concern himself only with painting while he was at Collioure. He also drew continually, and pondered the possibilities of transplanting the Fauve style of painting to sculpture. In his book on Matisse's sculptures, Albert Elsen defines these Fauve characteristics of sculpture as "foreshortening, informality and angularity of pose, absence of tasteful decorative accessories and the blatant immediacy with which the effects of the figure are propelled towards the viewer"; all these describe the *Reclining Nude, I* (page 12) that Matisse sculpted at Collioure during the summer of 1907. There in 1909 he began one of his most radical sculptures, *La Serpentine*. (He used as his point of departure a tawdry photograph of a naked model; live models were not to be found in Collioure.) Matisse was never idle. He rarely worked in water color, but in the summer of 1904 he had taken to it at the instigation of Signac, and when he was in Collioure in 1905 he painted a series of water colors, transparent washes of pure color on brilliant white paper. There is almost nothing there, and yet Matisse gives us a sense not only of deeply receding space but also of movement and reflected light.

Matisse and Derain were never again so close as in that summer of 1905. Nor did Matisse stick for long to the headlong exhilaration of pure Fauve painting. Fauvism for him was a necessary moment, not a lifelong vacation. But he kept on going to Collioure until the fateful summer of 1914 (after World War I he settled permanently in Nice), and memories of Collioure turn up in at least two of his greatest paintings. In his *Joy of Life* of 1905-6 (now at the Barnes Foundation in Merion, Pennsylvania) there are manifold echoes of Collioure: the scene is a clearing in the woods nearby, and the round dance in the background is the *sardana*; the imagined Arcadia is peopled with nude figures sketched, sculpted, or dreamed of in Collioure. Collioure is here mated with old master painting, with Matisse's memories of Titian, Bellini, Poussin, and Ingres, and is used as the pretext for formal inventions and manipulations that still retain their power to tease and provoke.

Joy of Life cannot be photographed in color (because of Barnes Foundation regulations), but for the other great echo of Collioure no such restriction exists. Matisse's *Dance* of 1909 (page 13), in the Museum of Modern Art in New York, is, once again, a transcription of the *sardana*. But it presents the *sardana* raised to the level of epic, with a self-generating energy remote from the stately circling of the local folk on the beach. What we see in the painting is still Collioure, but it is Collioure heightened and exalted, simplified and magnified, reduced and redoubled. It is to the actual fisherman's dance what Stravinsky's *Rite of Spring* is to the collection of Russian folk tunes that Stravinsky heard as a young man. In *Dance*, as in *Joy of Life*, an exceptional summer is immortalized.

Author of many books on modern art, John Russell, formerly of the London Times, *is now with the* New York Times. *His most recent article for* HO-RIZON *was "An Irresistible Force Called Max Ernst," in Autumn, 1973.*

In Matisse's Interior with Eggplants *of 1911, above, the pattern o*

e Collioure landscape outside the open window complements the exuberant patterns of decorative screens, tablecloths, curtains, and wallpaper inside the villa.

Biting
the Bullet
in
Ancient Rome

Peasants pay their taxes during the reign of Septimius Severus.

To curb inflation,
Diocletian used price controls—to some effect.
Then he found that
controlling the population worked even better

"Hurry and spend all the currency you have. Buy me goods of any kind at whatever price you find TETRADRACHMA them." So wrote a highly placed Roman to his business agent sometime around A.D. 300. The value of money was dropping relentlessly, and he wanted possessions, not cash. For the Roman Empire had been hit by inflation, and so violently that, to quote the emperor Diocletian, there were "increases in prices not only year by year, month by month, day by day, but almost hour by hour and minute by minute." He and his successors were eventually able to restore stability—but at a cost none of us would be willing to pay.

The economics of the Roman Empire is a baffling subject. Whatever accounts or records governments kept have almost totally disappeared. Only on rare occasions do historians mention a fact or figure that the economist finds useful,

and then merely incidentally. They report on scandals at court, the programs at the gladiatorial games, the fortunes of the legions; it would never enter their minds to discuss wages and prices. And so, at this remove, all we can do is guess at the overall state of the empire's economic health from the way things were going in general, how ably the emperors were governing, how wisely they were spending the imperial income, how troubled or peaceable their reigns were.

Luckily one part of the realm is an exception—Egypt. The valley of the Nile gets scant rain, and as a result, even such a fragile substance as papyrus can last for centuries, lying unharmed under the dry sand. Excavators have uncovered thousands of pieces of writing that date from the time when Egypt was ruled by Rome: letters (like the one cited above), notes, bills, receipts, memorandums, ledger sheets, legal instruments—the contents, as it were, of a vast archae-

ological trash basket. And here and there in this haphazard miscellany are enough crumbs of information to give us some idea of what was happening in the marketplace.

Even before any of these humble but enlightening documents had been unearthed, we were aware that, economically, the first two centuries of the Christian era were remarkable. It was the period Gibbon eulogizes in the opening words of his history as a golden age, the time when, as he puts it, "the Empire of Rome comprehended the fairest part of the earth, and the most civilized portion of mankind. The frontiers . . . were guarded by ancient renown and disciplined valor. The gentle but powerful influence of laws and manners had gradually cemented the union of the provinces. Their peaceful inhabitants enjoyed and abused the advantages of wealth and luxury." The provinces he refers to were the various states that Rome, in the course of centuries, had conquered and put under her rule, and they stretched from Spain to Syria and beyond. The emperors from their throne in the capital on the Tiber ruled this huge expanse with absolute authority—yet, during the first two centuries A.D., they exercised such restraint, and attended to the well-being of Rome's multifarious subjects with such success, that the Mediterranean world enjoyed the longest span of peace and political stability it ever had or would have.

These favoring circumstances gave birth to an unprecedented prosperity. Farms produced ample foodstuffs to feed the population. Artisans plied their crafts so profitably that many rose from the lower to the middle class. Traders flourished, particularly those dealing in luxury goods, for wealth was spread far wider than ever before, and greater and greater numbers were able to treat themselves to frills hitherto reserved for the lucky few. Ships of Greco-Roman merchants now made their way regularly down the eastern coast of Africa or across the Indian Ocean to satisfy the growing taste for ivory, gems, silks, exotic spices, and cosmetics. The coins

By LIONEL CASSON

Rome paid out for these costly items have been discovered as far away as Kenya, Ceylon, and China.

Anyone who has walked through Roman ruins dating from this period can see at a glance the tangible evidence of how well off people were, the remains of the expensive temples, public buildings, theatres, amphitheatres, baths, and aqueducts that they were able to build and maintain, not only in major cities but even in remote provincial towns. The documents found in Egypt provide an important additional piece of information that no ancient historian would ever mention or archaeological excavation could ever reveal: during this age the empire enjoyed the blessings not only of peace and prosperity but of stable prices. To be sure, the years of plenty inevitably drove prices up, but at a gentle, unhurried pace. Wheat, the commodity of commodities in a world for which bread truly was the staff of life, cost in Jesus' day about three drachmas an artab (roughly a bushel). It took a full century to climb to ten, half a century more to reach sixteen. Wine, oil, vegetables, wool—all the staples of life followed the same pattern, a gradual rise over a hundred and fifty years. (The tetradrachma, which equaled four drachmas, was used for actual payment. However, since the drachma was the money of account, prices here are indicated in drachmas.)

Historians today, with the gloomy vision of hindsight, tell us that clouds were already gathering over Rome's golden days at the very time things seemed brightest. The storms began to break shortly after the middle of the second century, when hordes of barbarians started to menace the northern frontiers and were turned back only by Marcus Aurelius' tireless leadership and the effectiveness of the Roman armies.

From the day the Roman Empire was founded, the power of its rulers rested on their control of the army, no matter how ingeniously they tried to disguise this. And even during the halcyon times of the first century, the soldiers every now and then had shown their muscle

and put a candidate of their own on the throne. Once they became the most important organ of the state, all that stood between it and destruction by invaders, they took over completely the role of kingmaker. When the emperor Septimius Severus, one of Rome's most successful military leaders, died in A.D. 211, the last word of advice he gave to his sons was to "stick together, pay the soldiers plenty, and forget about everything else."

The chief trouble was that the army itself could not stick together. There were always units ready to follow a commander willing to risk a try for the purple, some ready even to press a reluctant commander into risking such a try. The result was a never-ending series of civil wars, as the various claimants battled it out. And whoever won usually had to turn immediately to fending off the barbarian mobs that were now spilling over the northern borders at all points. A time came when Italy itself, the heartland of the empire, was threatened; the city of Rome received such a scare that, after having lived for seven hundred years with no defense wall, between A.D. 270 and 280 it rushed to completion the massive twelve-mile circuit that still can be seen in places today. To compound the difficulties, the rulers of Persia, having rejuvenated their nation, began marching westward, smashing Roman armies and even capturing an emperor on one occasion. Gaul, a rich and important province, broke away and stayed independent for fifteen years. And, as if all that was not enough, plague raged for a decade.

One inevitable result was that up and down the empire farmland either was ravaged or was abandoned as the men who worked it got killed off or were sucked into the army. The production of foodstuffs dropped, and with supply reduced but demand as strong as ever, prices, which for so long had risen only gently and gradually, took off. In the vanguard was the price of wheat. Around A.D. 250 it sold in Egypt, as mentioned above, for 16 drachmas an artab. Twenty years later it had leaped

to 200, an increase of more than 1,000 per cent. Other commodities went up almost as dramatically. "Pay the soldiers plenty," Septimius had counseled; with the staggering rise in costs, his successors were lucky if they could pay them at all. Yet they *had* to be paid—it was either that or be smothered under invading barbarians. In desperation, one emperor after another turned to the ancient world's equivalent of printing more money: they debased the coinage.

Hitherto the issues from Rome's mints had always contained a respectable amount of precious metal, particularly the silver issues that were the common coin of everyday transactions. During the second half of the third century the mints began to pour out bronze with just a silver wash, pieces that had hardly more intrinsic value than our dollar bills. Such a currency depends upon faith—but the emperors, buffeted by unceasing military and economic storms, were hardly in a position to take measures to inspire faith. The citizenry hurried to exchange what coin they had for tangible goods. Banks tried to get out of dealing with the ever more worthless stuff and had to be coerced. "My officials," announced a local administrator in Egypt, "have held a meeting in which they accuse the operators of banks dealing in currency exchange of closing their doors because of their unwillingness to accept the imperial coinage. I have been obliged to order all who own such banks to reopen and to accept and to exchange all coin. . . . This applies as well to those involved in business transactions of any kind."

Those involved in business transactions of any kind complied all right, but by raising prices at so quick a rate that, shortly before A.D. 300, there was rampaging inflation throughout the empire. Egyptian wheat, after its initial leap from 16 to 200 drachmas an artab, by the year 300 had soared to more than 1,300; fourteen years later it sold for 10,000, twenty years after that for 84,000, and sometime after 344 a sale is recorded at the astronomical figure of 2,000,000. Beans, which for centuries cost no more than 6 drachmas an artab, in A.D. 308 cost 900. In 217 donkeys had sold for 400 drachmas; in 277 the price was up to 3,800 and by 309 to 15,000. In A.D. 280 a cavalryman had been able to buy a horse for 1,300 drachmas; in 307 an officer of a Roman unit stationed in Egypt had to lay out 780,000.

Those who had any gold or silver hoarded it in time-honored fashion by burying it in the ground; those who had only the now nearly valueless coins were wiped out, like the Germans after World War I who found themselves turning over the equivalent of a year's income to buy a loaf of bread. Among the pieces of writing of this age that have been recovered is a list of the questions people were putting to the fortunetellers. "Will I become a beggar?" they were asking. "Will my property be sold off at auction?" "Will I become a runaway?" "Will I be caught running away?"

During these years Diocletian, ruthless but supremely able, was on the throne. He had put down several rivals, beaten back barbarians and Persians, reformed the army and administration. That still left inflation to deal with. In A.D. 301 he tried the solution so frequently urged today, price controls. He issued an edict that set the maximum price for every conceivable service or object of exchange, from a pound of grapes (4 drachmas) to a pound of gold (200,000), from pitchforks (16

drachmas each) to dyed silk (600,000 a pound), from the hire of sewer cleaners (100 drachmas a day plus keep) to that of trial lawyers (4,000 a case).

The penalty for buying or selling at higher figures, or for just withholding from the market, was no mere fine or jail sentence, but death or exile. Diocletian thought that nasty profiteers were causing all the trouble, men afflicted with the "unbridled passion for money-grabbing," and that once they were brought into line the problem would be solved. Moreover, being as absolute a monarch as any the world has ever known (it was he who introduced groveling as the official way to greet a Roman emperor), he had no need to trim his sails to the wishes of vested interests or the ideas of a congress or be overnice about due process. Yet a contemporary reports that soon after the controls went into effect, "nothing appeared on the market because of fear, and prices soared much higher"—in other words, hoarding and a black market. "In the end," he adds, "after many people had lost their lives, it became absolutely necessary to repeal the law." The writer, as it happens, was a Christian and hence had scant love for Diocletian, a savage persecutor of the growing sect, but the sales figures in the documents from Egypt grimly confirm what he says.

Another way of attacking the problem turned out in the long run to be

more successful. Diocletian's predecessors, in their frantic efforts to keep their soldiers fed and clothed, had now and then collected taxes in kind instead of in currency. Diocletian made this the standard practice. He devised a system, not particularly fair but easy to apply and enforce, whereby everybody paid taxes in units of wheat, barley, meat, wine, oil, timber, labor. At the same time he switched the pay of the army and the civil service from sums of money to rations of commodities.

So far, so good—but how to extract the amounts needed from a populace that years of turmoil had thinned in numbers, impoverished, and demoralized? Diocletian went about this in two ways. First, he institutionalized a form of gouging that his predecessors had already been driven to use. After each community had been notified what commodities it was liable for and how much, the local administration, consisting naturally of the wealthiest members, was charged with the collection—and, if what they gathered in fell short of the assessed totals, they had to make up the difference themselves. Second, since in the face of ever-rising taxes the small farmers, especially the greater number who worked the soil as tenants, had a lamentable tendency to abandon their lands and run off in a desperate search for greener pastures, he decreed that people were not to move from the place

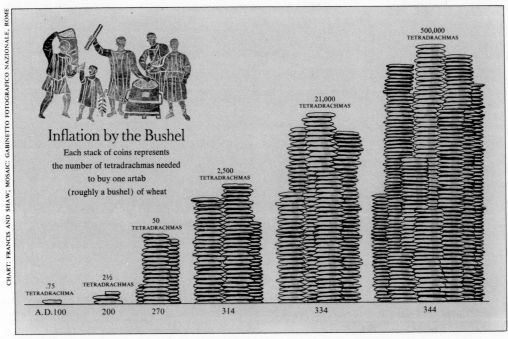

CHART: FRANCIS AND SHAW; MOSAIC: GABINETTO FOTOGRAFICO NAZIONALE, ROME

Inflation by the Bushel

Each stack of coins represents
the number of tetradrachmas needed
to buy one artab
(roughly a bushel) of wheat

.75 TETRADRACHMA
2½ TETRADRACHMAS
50 TETRADRACHMAS
2,500 TETRADRACHMAS
21,000 TETRADRACHMAS
500,000 TETRADRACHMAS

A.D. 100   200   270   314   334   344

During the second century A.D., when prices started to increase, government distribution centers (like the one in the inset mosaic from Ostia) offered wheat at fixed prices or gave it away free to the needy.

where they had been registered at birth. Subsequent legislation spelled this out with brutal clarity:

Tenant farmers . . . shall be bound by the rule of geographical origin, and, though they appear to have the status of freeborn, shall nevertheless be considered slaves of the land itself to which they are born, and shall have no right to go off where they like or to change their location, but the landowner shall enjoy his right over them, [exercising] the care of a patron and the power of a master.

There was no lack of land; Diocletian saw to it that hands were available to do the planting and harvesting.

Throughout the empire, though there was still a goodly number of smallholders, the bulk of the arable land had been gathered into large estates. This made the collection of taxes in foodstuffs instead of money all the easier: Diocletian's revenue office simply had to calculate the grand total each was responsible for. Many of them were vast tracts encompassing whole villages and towns; at one time, we are told, half of what is today Tunisia and the eastern part of Algeria was owned by six families. Moreover, most tended to get still bigger, for time and again independent farmers, driven to the wall by unrelenting taxation but unwilling to take the drastic remedy of running away to escape it, took refuge under the protection of the nearest powerful landowner, turning their fields over to him and becoming his tenants. Such big holdings became not only larger, but steadily more self-sufficient, including within their embrace craftsmen of all kinds to provide whatever services were needed, sometimes even squads of armed men as the landlord's private bodyguard and police force. When Diocletian tied the tenants to the soil, he set in motion the process that was to convert these estates into the serf-manned feudal manors of the Middle Ages.

Taxes in kind have to be transported and processed before they can be issued as rations to soldiers and government clerks. The question was how to do this without paying out cash. Roman traders and craftsmen had long been organized

Septimius Severus

Diocletian

Constantine I

The empire versus inflation: Septimius devalued the coinage and raised taxes; Diocletian imposed price controls and tied the peasant to the land; Constantine "solved" the problem by instituting a totalitarian state.

into associations, but these were ancient versions of our marching and chowder societies: they were purely social, not for business or trade. The harassed emperors of the third century seized upon them as a way of getting services at reduced or no cost; from mere social groups they were transformed into government instruments compelled to do the bidding of the state.

The associations of carters in the various towns were made responsible for transport of government goods on land, the associations of shippers for overseas transport, the associations of bakers for turning government grain into bread, and so on. And, just as Diocletian had tied the peasant to his soil, he and his followers tied the traders and craftsmen to their organizations: they were forbidden to change occupation, and their heirs were required to carry on their obligation. It goes without saying that the same restrictions were placed on soldiers, whose services the state needed more than any other: they were bound to the colors, and their sons had to follow in their footsteps.

In the few areas where the state found no association to do its work, it did the work itself. State-run factories were set up to turn out weapons and armor for the troops, and state-run linen mills and woolen mills to turn out clothing for the civil service as well as the troops. There were still a few things that the emperors, willy-nilly, had to buy with money. By various measures they methodically

pried loose whatever gold and silver people had managed to hoard and used this to mint new issues of perfectly sound coins, particularly gold ones. Constantine, who followed Diocletian after a short interval, when he came out in favor of Christianity, helped himself to the treasures in the pagan temples, and this put ample stocks of bullion in his hands.

In effect, what Diocletian and his successors achieved was the by-passing of the free market where the fires of inflation were raging. In the process they drastically reduced its extent. The government had all along been the empire's biggest customer. Now it became very much bigger than ever before—and, at the same time, removed its trade almost completely from the marketplace: it collected its own foodstuffs and materials, paid its personnel with what it collected, made its own munitions. The growth of more and larger landed estates, all for the most part self-sufficient, reduced the extent of inflation still further. Indeed, most of what was left of any importance in the private sector, and therefore subject to the laws of supply and demand, was the feeding and furnishing of the urban populations— and not even all of that, since the poor of Rome, Constantinople, and certain other major centers were fed by government handouts. Inflation still smoldered on this limited terrain, but the emperors were not at all bothered: what money accounts they had were kept in the new inflation-proof gold coinage. By the end of the fourth century, with scant fuel to feed on, the last flames of inflation flickered out.

So, along with a host of other problems, Rome solved its inflation by controlling not merely prices but the entire lives of most of its subjects, locking them forever into fixed places in the socioeconomic order. Rome solved it, in short, by transforming itself into a totalitarian state as rigid and all-pervasive as any the world has known.

Lionel Casson wrote on the folkways of ancient health seekers in our Spring issue.

A SEASON IN OMAN

This ancient seafaring nation
entered the twentieth century by way of
the fourteenth. The old life
was harsh and limiting. The new has
brought the usual modern
trappings, including a guerrilla war

By DAVID HOLDEN

In 1964 Qabus bin Said, above, then heir apparent,
was imprisoned by his father, the sultan of Oman,
in a palace five hundred desert miles from Muscat,
right, the capital. Qabus overthrew him in 1970 and
began prodding the country out of its long dark age.

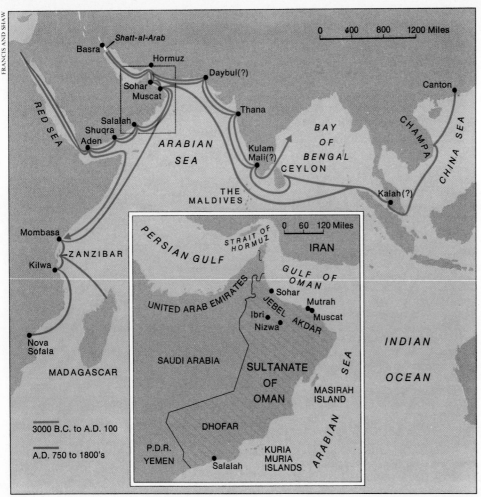

The sea is the key to Oman's history. From the third millennium B.C. to the 1800's Omani seamen routinely sailed these Indian Ocean routes. The legendary Sinbad may well have been an Omani.

The Arab Sultanate of Oman has never, in modern times, been one of the world's familiar places. Until a few years ago, probably not one in a hundred people outside the Arabian peninsula had heard of it, despite its command of one of the crucial tanker routes. When at last Oman emerged from obscurity some twenty years ago, even senior officials at the United Nations had to consult the atlas to assure themselves of its existence.

Stuck at the far southeast corner of Arabia, between the Indian Ocean and the Persian Gulf, Oman has long been about as isolated from modern global affairs as any place could be. Even the outbreak of political rebellion in the 1950's and the discovery of oil in the 1960's did not seem at first to disturb its seclusion. In the hands of an old, determined, and crafty ruler who was resolved to let nothing change his or his people's ways, the country lingered on for years in apparent innocence of the

twentieth century and all its works. Only in 1970, when the old sultan was replaced in a palace coup by his more enlightened son, did Oman open its doors to the modern world and thereby allow itself to be propelled, in the flicker of a historical eyelash, from the fourteenth century to the twentieth.

The change is still so recent that Oman—known until 1970 as Muscat and Oman—still retains the enigmatic image of a country that the rest of the world cannot quite place. One reason is that its oil resources are merely modest, producing no more than a billion dollars' worth of crude a year even at current prices. Although this is wealth undreamed of compared to Oman's previous poverty, it is little enough to be spread among some seven hundred thousand people scattered across a country roughly the size of Britain, and it is scarcely more than a pittance beside the vast revenues of the major Middle Eastern oil powers.

But Oman nowadays has other claims to the world's attention. For one thing, it overlooks the narrow passage between the Indian Ocean and the gulf called the Strait of Hormuz, described by the shah of Iran as the jugular vein of the modern world. Oman also suffers Arabia's only current war. In its southern province of Dhofar a small but tenacious guerrilla campaign has been conducted for more than a decade now by an organization called the Popular Front for the Liberation of the Arab Gulf. Its leaders proclaim their intention not only to overthrow the sultanate and all it stands for but also to free all the sheikdoms of the gulf from the clutches of the "capitalist-imperialists" and their "puppet" rulers. Small as the sultan's war is, it is expensive, eating up more than half the Omani national income.

To suppress the rebellion the sultan has brought to his aid a mixed bag of foreign troops and mercenaries whose presence gives his kingdom a place in the front line of contemporary ideological conflict. They include Iranian ground troops experiencing their first taste of combat, hard-bitten Jordanian army officers and pilots from King Hussein's forces, British officers transferred by their government from duties in Germany and Northern Ireland, and retired British military men doubling their pensions with a spot of soldierly adventure on the sultan's payroll. Before long they may even include a few Americans, for discreet approaches have been made in the past year or two to enable the United States to expand an existing British air and communications base on the sultan's island of Masirah, off the Dhofar coast, to counter what the Pentagon regards as the growing Russian threat in the Indian Ocean.

The war serves a typically modern purpose: it is helping to usher into Oman the characteristic revolution of money, political change, and technological advance that has already transformed so much of the contemporary world. In the process, after an interval of a century and more, it is once again putting Oman on the political and

BULL AND DANCER: WENDELL PHILLIPS, *Qataban and Sheba*, 1955

economic map, recalling several earlier periods when, through geographic circumstance, Oman was the flourishing middleman of seaborne trade carried on between India, China, and Africa and the successive civilizations of Mesopotamia and Persia.

Blessed by their strategic position at the mouth of the Persian Gulf and by the regular, annual swing of the monsoon winds, the people of Oman have always been involved in maritime adventure. The monsoon—an Arabic word meaning "seasonal"—is the most predictable of the sailor's winds. In summer it blows from the southwest, filling the sails of any vessel bound north or east. In winter its course is reversed. Blowing from the northeast, it carries those same vessels back again, so that in a span of twelve months an experienced captain can run before the wind for five thousand miles each way—say, from Africa to China and back—with little more fuss than an ordinary yachtsman might make in sailing a dinghy around his local bay.

Two thousand years ago the Greeks and Romans harnessed the monsoon's obliging characteristics to carry their ships to and from India. Long before that, however, sailors of the Persian Gulf had begun to learn the monsoon's uses. Running regularly from the Sumerian ports of Mesopotamia to India and back, they established themselves as ocean traders as much as five thousand years ago. Much later, their medieval Arab successors ranged still more widely in the same way. Sitting at the fulcrum of the monsoon's seasonal swings, they rode it far to both east and west, to China in one direction and Africa in the other, and turned Oman's harbors into the home of some of the world's most skillful sea captains and more irrepressible pirates.

The monsoon was important in another way, too. It brought fertility to this far corner of Arabia. Sweeping the inland mountains of Oman with summer rain clouds from the Indian Ocean, it helped to create green, watered terraces that are like a small vision of paradise amid the surrounding desert.

Domed tomb

Bronze bull   *Female dancer*

Oman has been inhabited ever since the Paleolithic Age. Although only a few archaeologists have thus far visited the region, there have already been some important finds, such as the burial site above, built in the third millennium B.C., the bronze bull (date uncertain), and the second-century dancer.

Evidence of humanity, dating back as much as thirty thousand years, has been discovered in these mountains, and the burial chambers of settled communities recently excavated there have been ascribed to the third millennium B.C.

In antiquity, in the highlands beyond the Dhofar coast, the monsoon's misty passage provided just the right climate for the growth of the frankincense tree. As the demand for incense grew among priests and magicians throughout the pagan world, Dhofar established itself as the most prolific and accessible source. It was a trade as lucrative in its time as today's oil business, for, after gold, incense was the most coveted of all commodities. Herodotus reports that each year two and a half tons of incense were burned at the temple of Baal at Babylon, and all of it probably came from Oman. On the proceeds of their virtual monopoly, the geographer Pliny said, the people of southern Arabia became the richest in all the world.

But nothing lasts forever. Early in the Christian era, as pagan temples began to close and the trade routes to Europe

withered, south Arabian wealth declined. Now it was the turn of the Persians to cross the gulf, extend their power into Oman, and establish a tradition of Persian intervention that still alarms Arab leaders as they contemplate the growing military power of the shah of Iran. After the Persians came the Prophet, and with Islam's victory Oman began to acquire, in the seventh century A.D., the character that still shapes the traditional aspects of its life. In many ways it was—and is—a singularly dour and introspective character, for in the schisms that soon overtook the vast new Moslem empire the mountains of Oman became a fortress of the puritanical Ibadite sect. Founded at the end of the seventh century by a learned doctor named Abdullah ibn Ibadh, the movement forbade alcohol, tobacco, and even music. In emphasizing the sanctity of Moslem law, it did, however, encourage a tradition of minute Islamic scholarship—it was an Ibadite of Oman who produced the first known Arabic dictionary—and in its determination that all men should be treated equally under God it insisted upon choosing religious leaders by election, a custom unknown to other Moslems.

The Ibadites enjoyed their greatest success in North Africa, where their peculiar version of the faith became for a time the established religion of the Berber tribes. (Some of the remote villages in the Atlas Mountains still cling to it.) But it was in the isolated glens of the mountains of Oman that the Ibadites were destined to survive most tenaciously and to reject most fiercely the corruptions of the world.

Even in Arabia, never a land to fear excessive piety, the Ibadites of Oman were renowned for their pride and exclusiveness in the name of Allah. The British traveler Bertram Thomas, visiting the fringes of their territory in the 1930's, found them a thoroughly tiresome lot who even showed distress at the sound of drums during the burial of a Negro slave:

"God forgive them!" murmured the sanctimonious Omani at my side.

"Drums aren't acceptable to you?" I questioned.

"No, nor pipes; but these are slaves and know no better."

"Yet the Muqabil tribe in Oman have pipes?" I said.

"Yes! But they are Sunnis. We are Ibadhis, and in Ibadhi Oman we forbid these instruments of the devil."

Such a bleak morality could hardly help conflicting with the far more worldly attitudes that flourished along the Oman coast, where successive waves of Arab, Persian, Indian, and European merchants mingled in a society of commerce and corruption. That is why Oman's history is a perennial drum roll of factionalism and fanaticism spilling out of the interior to challenge the worldly ways and corrupting rule of the coast—a conflict that was echoed in the Omani risings of the 1950's and is even now reflected in some of the attitudes behind the fighting in Dhofar. One result of this incessant lawlessness has been that Oman possesses probably the world's finest assortment of medieval stone and mud forts, for until twenty years ago no village dared exist without one.

The early centuries of Moslem ascendancy in the Middle East brought new stimulus to the Oman coast. A full eight hundred years before Columbus, Oman merchants were the first to link the Moslem empire of the Abbassides with the great T'ang dynasty in China, sailing more than five thousand miles from the Shatt-al-Arab to Canton and back. By the tenth century, what is now the crumbling, mud-walled town of Sohar, a hundred miles northwest of Muscat, had become the Omani capital and was one of the biggest ports on the fringes of the Indian Ocean.

Yet when Vasco da Gama rounded Africa and opened the sea route from Europe to India it was the turn of the Portuguese to dominate the gulf trade and the Oman coast. For a hundred and fifty years they made Muscat their trading center, and the great twin forts they

During the eighteenth and nineteenth centuries much of Oman's wealth came from the slave trade, which flourished under Tippu Tib, a brutal Afro-Arab trader, and Said bin Sultan, whose daughter, opposite, once declared, "Negroes are very lazy. . . . nothing remains but the lash." Above, slaves from Zanzibar, Africa's slavery capital, after their rescue in 1884 by the crew of H.M.S. London.

Tippu Tib   *Said bin Sultan*

built above its harbor made it thereafter the key to Omani power. Only when Portuguese strength declined did that of the Omanis again advance. Characteristically, the resurgence came from the Ibadites of the interior. Scandalized as ever by the corruptions of the coast, they killed the last Portuguese defender of Muscat in 1650 and by 1700 made Oman once more the greatest independent power of the Arabian peninsula.

For much of the eighteenth century the Omani sultans were rulers to be reckoned with in many of the lands east of Suez. Exploiting the monsoon winds, their ships carried silk from China, spices from India, and slaves from all the territories of east Africa. In Arab hands, as in those of the Europeans on Africa's western coast, the traffic in slaves was a cruel but immensely profitable business that built Omani fortunes as surely as it wasted African lives. On its profits the sultans became almost as rich as the south Arabians had once become on the incense monopoly.

They also made themselves patrons of a cultural revival that united Indian and Arab skills in some of the finest craftsmanship in Arabia. Omani silverwork, in massive bracelets, filigreed necklaces, and beautifully worked dagger hilts and scabbards, was renowned throughout the peninsula. Omani coffeepots and intricately brass-bound wooden sea chests were—and still are—recognized as among the best of their kind. Their merchants' houses, too, had an impressive elegance. In Muscat, Zanzibar, and several now-neglected towns of the African shore they can still be seen—tall, cool, thick walled, and narrow windowed, their galleried courtyards shut away from the world by carved doors of the liveliest workmanship.

To protect all this from rivals and pirates, the Omani sultans also acquired a substantial navy containing, according to some optimistic accounts, no fewer than seventy-five ships of the line. Thus, by the end of the eighteenth century, when the British sought allies to protect their growing Indian trade from European rivals, the sultan of Muscat, as the Omani ruler was known by then, was their first choice. In 1798, with Napoleon already in Egypt and India in his dreams, Britain signed a treaty of friendship with the sultan—its first imperial agreement with any Arabian ruler. It was a distinctly one-sided affair, implicitly affirming British supremacy and excluding all other powers from Muscat. The treaty grandly noted:

As improper reports of a tendency to interrupt the existing harmony and create misunderstanding between the States have gone abroad . . . , we, actuated by sentiments of reciprocal friendship, agree that an English gentleman of respectability . . . shall always reside at the port of Muscat, and be an Agent through whom all intercourse between the States shall be conducted, in order that the actions of each government may be fairly and justly stated, and that no opportunity may be offered to designing men, who are

Saiyidah Bibi Salme, minus the customary Arab veil

Oman's command of the Strait of Hormuz and the Gulf of Oman has long prompted covetous thoughts and predatory acts. Above, a nineteenth-century water color of Fort Mirani, built in Muscat in 1588 by the Portuguese, who sacked the city and for a century and more controlled Oman's coast.

ever eager to promote dissensions, and that the friendship . . . may remain unshook till the end of time, and till the sun and moon have finished their revolving career.

In time, British curtailment of piracy and the slave trade severed the sinews of Oman's commerce, and when the new nineteenth-century steamships mocked the monsoon and by-passed Oman's ports, even the skills of Oman's sailors at last became irrelevant. By 1833, when the sultan was permitted by his British allies to sign a treaty of friendship with the United States—the first formal agreement ever made between America and any Middle Eastern power—Oman was already a shadow of its eighteenth-century self. Not long afterward, as British hegemony was consolidated everywhere around the Indian Ocean, Oman turned in upon itself again and went quietly and conclusively to sleep.

It was that sleep from which I found the place just beginning to awaken when I first went there two decades ago. The year was 1957. For the whole of the preceding century most of Oman might as well not have existed as far as the great, wide world was concerned. It was July, and up in the baking mountains in the heart of Oman—called the Jebel Akdar, the Green Mountain—schisms that had racked the sultanate for centuries had flared into life again. In scale and style

they seemed insignificant: a few hundred crudely armed tribesmen raising a flag of rebellion against the sultan, much as their forefathers had done many times before. But this time the ancient conflicts were entangled with contemporary ambitions. Excited by the arrival of the first oil prospectors in the interior of Oman a few years earlier and inflamed for political reasons by the governments of Egypt and Saudi Arabia, the tribesmen had sensed new horizons. Their quarrels therefore had a new dimension.

Alarmed, the sultan called British troops to his aid, in fulfillment of the old Omani-British alliance. Then, amid inevitable allegations of "imperialism" and "aggression," the little tribal uprising was elevated to the status of a "national liberation movement" and what was soon to be known as "the Oman question" appeared on the agenda of the United Nations and became a hardy perennial of international dispute.

As a British correspondent in the Middle East at the time, I had a small but inescapable role in this assault upon the last remaining bastion of Arabian tradition. I was ordered off at once to hammer upon the sultan's doors and try to discover what was really going on. It was a difficult task, for the sultan was not accustomed to opening his doors to importuning journalists—or, for that

matter, to anyone else—and he was even less disposed to do so now that he was in trouble. The combined weight of Fleet Street and the British Foreign Office, with the American State Department pressing discreetly in the background, was required to get me, in company with an American colleague, into Oman. But at length, in an elderly aircraft of the Royal Air Force, we made a perilous landing one afternoon on a gravel strip in the mountains near Muscat and stepped straight out into some other, older time.

Never before or since have I experienced anything quite as disorienting as those first few days in the Oman capital. Muscat seemed literally the embodiment of another era; our aircraft might as well have been a time machine. Partly, no doubt, this was an illusion induced by the city's peculiar physical isolation and its beastly summer climate. It lies cramped at the head of a narrow, cliff-bound inlet off the Gulf of Oman, hemmed in by hills of the utmost barrenness. "The whole country round this place," wrote an earlier British visitor, a certain William Francklin of the Honourable East India Company, who arrived on New Year's Day in 1787, "is one continued solid rock, without a blade of grass, or any kind of verdure to be seen." So it is, and in July (as Francklin, lucky fellow, could only guess) that rock seems to focus the punishing sun of Arabia like a magnifying glass upon the dusty alleyways of the little town. Indeed, in Francklin's day, and long after, the few foreign residents unfortunate enough to live in Muscat used to wrap themselves in wet sheets and sleep on their roofs on summer nights—a practice sometimes held responsible for the foreigners' alarmingly high death rate.

By the time I arrived, however, most of the score or so of Europeans in the town had acquired electric ceiling fans and learned the use of salt tablets. In the European house where I stayed (for there was not a single hotel then throughout the length and breadth of Oman) the servants who brought my sundown drink in one hand invariably offered me a dish of salt tablets with the other, much as elsewhere they might have extended peanuts or a cheese dip. But such rudimentary amenities did little to blunt the stupefying impact of the heat. Passing the days in a torpid, almost trancelike state, I felt myself a sort of Rip Van Winkle in reverse, caught up in a somnolent, historical hallucination.

Though Muscat was by then a great anachronism, it possessed a seductive and romantic charm. Each evening, at the two gates in the town's mud wall, guards would slowly heave shut the great iron-studded doors. Thereafter, until dawn, no one could pass either in or out without written authority from the town governor, nor could anybody move about Muscat's streets without carrying a lantern with a lighted flame. A plain electric torch was not permitted as a substitute. It was, I was told, too easily switched on or off at moments of secrecy or emergency. Besides, a big one would make a more effective club than a lantern in the hands of anyone bent on mischief.

But this sort of thing was only the more engaging aspect of a prevailing medievalism that laid harsh restrictions of every kind upon Oman. By 1957, in fact, the Omani sultan of the day—one Said bin Taimur Al bu Said by name—was just about the most reactionary and isolationist ruler in all Arabia. The thirteenth sultan of the Al bu Said dynasty, Said bin Taimur was a strange and quirky man, combining a twinkling, soft-spoken, and sophisticated manner with natural cunning and a high degree of ruthlessness. He had been educated at college in India under the British raj and was a regular visitor to London, yet he was the only Arabian ruler who still kept a personal retinue of slaves. I met some of them when they were at length released, after their master's deposition in 1970, and discovered that one or two had been so cut off from normal human contacts that they had almost

lost the power of speech. Shambling uncertainly into the sunlight of unaccustomed freedom, they were potent symbols of the sultan's entire people, who were kept for as long as he remained in power in a state of more or less universal ignorance, illiteracy, bigotry, and ill-health, utterly out of touch with the outside world and the twentieth century.

The sultan's personal authority was virtually absolute and the joyless prohibitions of a puritanical Islam were rigidly enforced: nobody could smoke, dance, play music in public, or—unless he was one of the tiny band of privileged foreigners—drink any alcohol. Apart from the traditional Koranic schools where children learned only to chant the Moslem holy book by heart, no child could go to school unless the sultan ap-

Portugal's Affonso

Persia's Nadir Shah

proved, an honor so rarely conferred that there were only three small modern schools in the whole of Oman.

Medical treatment was equally discouraged, the only modern hospital in the country being a tiny American mission establishment that was obliged to do most of its good by stealth. Nobody could open a business or build a house, or even so much as repair one, without the sultan's personal permission. Nor could anyone enter the kingdom or leave it, or even travel about in it, without his direct authority. And since the sultan chose to spend most of his time in total seclusion in Salalah, five hundred miles from Muscat and most of his people, that authority was uncommonly hard to seek, let alone secure.

The sultan's apologists attributed his obstinate attitudes to his father, who had left him a bankrupt treasury in the 1930's, when he had taken over as a young man. In pursuing the elusive goal of solvency ever after, he had developed, it was said, habits of deep conservatism and miserly penny-pinching that he could never outgrow. If so, they had become obsessions by the time I met him, for although he had succeeded by then in accumulating a little money— and was close to receiving a good deal more—he resolutely rejected all proposals for its use in bettering the decrepit condition of his kingdom.

His determination to keep Oman free from the modern world's infections extended with bizarre logic even to his immediate family. His brother, Tariq, was forced to smuggle his sons out of the country in order to get them into a proper school, and the sultan's own son, Qabus, was eighteen before his father was at last persuaded by the British to let him leave Oman and prepare himself for his responsibilities as a future ruler. After a crash course in elementary education with British tutors, Qabus spent some time as an officer cadet at Sandhurst, the British military academy, and finally put in a year's service

England's Neil Innes (right)

The shah of Iran

Among the many outsiders who have played roles in Oman are Affonso de Albuquerque, who seized Muscat in 1507; Nadir Shah, who invaded Oman in 1737; Foreign Minister Neil Innes, who helped Sultan Said bin Taimur (with Innes above) crush a rebellion in 1957; and Mohammed Riza Pahlavi, who now trains some of his forces there.

29

with a Scottish regiment in Germany. In his early twenties he returned loyally to his father's side. But Sultan Said, seeing his son as more of a threat than a help-meet, reacted in truly autocratic fashion. He locked him up in a suite in his whitewashed palace near the Indian Ocean's shore, with nothing more than a phonograph and a pile of records to keep him company.

Yet in fairness to Sultan Said it must be said that, whatever his failings, he and his people seemed to understand each other, at least until his final para-noiac years. His ways and theirs had, after all, a certain cultural coherence. They shared the same roots and tradi-tions, embedded in a thousand years or more of Oman's history. It was their misfortune that they happened to share, too, the impoverished end of an era. At several other times in the Omani past they might have prospered together as representatives of one of Arabia's most powerful kingdoms, blessed by the unique combination of strategic posi-tion and the regular arrival of the beneficent monsoon wind.

As it turned out, it was only a matter of time before Sultan Said bin Taimur was compelled to abandon his position as the last of the Arabian Canutes, vainly trying to stem the tide of the mod-ern world. In July, 1970, the end arrived at last. He was overthrown by his own son, Qabus, discreetly aided by his old British friends, to whom, by that time, he had become an intolerable embar-rassment.

The occasion took me back once more to Oman. This time I was wel-comed as I had never been before, as a representative of everything the old sul-tan had rejected. Suddenly all the re-strictions were abandoned, all the secret places were unveiled, as from all over Oman tribesmen arrived to greet the new sultan. Day after day and night after night they danced through the streets in a dementia of joy. Sweat soaked their thin cotton robes but still they did not stop. They blew on reed pipes through bulbous cheeks and rattled goatskin drums as if the prohibi-

Six years after Qabus's coup, the twentieth century—including television, cars, and su-permarkets—is sweeping into Oman. Omani children (opposite), who until 1970 studied only the Koran, now take other courses, too.

tions of Ibadism had never been heard of. Men stamped and shouted, women trilled and swayed. Ancient rifles crackled, silver daggers flashed, and gold teeth glinted, laughing in the sun. In liv-ing memory—and probably far longer —Muscat had never seen anything like this moment of jubilation and release after a generation of deprivation and a century of sleep.

Yet even as the noise rose and fell, it was plain that the euphoria could not last, for the life from which it sprang was ending, too. I was listening to a dirge as well as a celebration.

The signs of irrevocable change are legion now and, as always in such cir-cumstances, much that is socially hope-ful is mingled with much that is tawdry and corrupt. New schools, medical clinics, houses, roads, and agricultural centers have transformed the lives and expectations of thousands of Omani families. At Oman's new international airport the jets roar in daily with fresh cargoes of oilmen and bankers eager to lead Oman into their version of the twentieth-century paradise. Radios and color television sets bring global news and images to people who only yester-day could see no farther than the neigh-boring tribe.

But as the harsh constraints of cen-

turies are lifted, so do the virtues of the past decay. Greed replaces Oman's traditional generosity, the security of ritual surrenders to the confusions of freedom, and much that is worst in the modern world is eagerly sought as the best by people who are making their first experiments in choice. Every big new contract has its payoff, each additional school and hospital lines somebody's pocket. Needless Cadillacs multiply among the newly rich, and on the lovely Muscat waterfront, undisturbed for centuries, Sultan Qabus has erected a gimcrack tycoon's palace that looks like an oriental Disneyland.

Oman's traditions of craftsmanship are abandoned or preserved only as curiosities. Cars, wrist watches, radios, television sets, and record players are everybody's status symbols now. And as the experts fly into Oman, the Omanis fly out, panting for the once forbidden pleasures of foreign casinos, strip clubs, and call girls.

They leave behind a society in total flux. It had to happen, of course, and though there is always some sadness when an old way of life crumbles abruptly, Oman's transformation de-serves few regrets. The old life there was harsh and deeply limiting. Far better today's open and comparatively afflu-ent horizons, with all their risks and cor-ruptions, than yesterday's drab, impris-oning certainties.

In any case, if we try to take the long view, we may see Oman's current awakening as an event in many ways more in keeping with its national past than the century of sleep that has just ended. For on the twentieth-century tide of oil and politics, the Sultanate of Oman has been restored not merely to a measure of physical wealth and health but also to its oldest and most tradi-tional international role—as gatekeeper to that most vital of all trade routes, the one between the Middle Eastern heart-land and the oceans of the world.

David Holden, a correspondent who has long specialized in Middle Eastern af-fairs, is the author of Farewell to Arabia.

When Paris Was a City for the Young

Students, painters, intellectuals, journalists, grisettes—all were there, along with a young German poet who recorded the epoch of creative ferment between one revolution and the next

"If anyone asks you how I'm getting on here," Heinrich Heine wrote to the pianist Ferdinand Hiller, "tell him, like a fish in the water. Or rather, tell people that when one fish in the sea asks another how he's getting on, the reply is: 'Like Heine in Paris.'" It was the springtime of French romanticism. Paris had welcomed *le célèbre auteur allemand, docteur Heine* (as *Le Globe* called him) with open arms when he arrived from Germany in May, 1831: indeed, rarely have a writer and a city been so obviously destined for each other.

"I arrived in Paris at a very remarkable moment in history," Heine remembered afterward. "The French people had just enacted their July revolution amid the applause of the whole world." This time the revolution had not been followed by scenes of terror and the tumbling of eminent heads into waiting baskets. Instead Heine found a city made for young poets.

Paris delighted me, particularly on account of the air of gaiety that makes itself felt in everything, and that exercises its influence on even the gloomiest spirits. It's very curious: Paris is the theatre wherein the greatest tragedies of human history have been performed. . . . The spectator of these Parisian tragedies has, however, an experience similar to my own at the Porte Saint-Martin Theatre, where I saw a performance of Alexandre

Heinrich Heine, above, arrived in Paris in May, 1831, to find the ultimate romantic city. Opposite, in a painting by Victor Jean Nicolle, is the Ile de la Cité and the Left Bank at that time, as viewed from the Louvre.

Dumas's *Tour de Nesle.* I happened to be seated behind a lady who wore a hat made of rose-colored gauze; this hat was so broad that it completely interposed itself between me and the stage, so that I witnessed the whole tragedy through a screen of red gauze, and thus all the horrors of the drama appeared to me in the gayest rose-colored light. In Paris, too, there is such a rose-colored atmosphere to brighten for the spectator the gloom of its tragedies. Even the terrors of his own heart, which the traveler brings with him to Paris, lose their brooding pain. His

griefs are wonderfully lightened. In the air of Paris all wounds heal more quickly than elsewhere; there is something in the atmosphere as generous, as benign, as gracious as the people themselves.

These remarks are a thinly veiled allusion to the healing therapy his own broken heart had undergone in Paris. He had arrived with a brooding pain of considerable intensity, still in the throes of an unrequited passion for his blonde, flirtatious cousin Amalie, daughter of the Hamburg banker Salomon Heine. Although he was only thirty-three at the time, he had already been a literary celebrity for several years, thanks to his poems *Die Lorelei, On Wings of Song,* and a dozen others. His own mixed feelings toward his new-found fame are summed up with a typically ironic smile in the poem in which he encounters a brown-eyed lass who asks him who he is and what ails him. He answers:

I am a German poet
Known throughout Germany,
And when they mention the best-known names
They have to talk of me.

And that which ails me, little one,
Ails a-many in Germany;
And when they talk of men's bitterest pains
They must mention my agony.

Heine's sarcasm in prose, however,

Delacroix's Liberty

STREET FIGHTING: JULY, 1830

Delacroix, though bored by politics, was stirred by the Revolution of 1830, when Parisians took to the barricades to protest Royalist decrees. The artist even watched some of the fighting and, as an expression of his love and concern for France, painted *Liberty Leading the People*, with Liberty as half goddess and half woman of the streets. A preliminary sketch for the work is above.

Bourgeois, students, and workers clash with soldiers in the rue de Rohan on July 29, 1830.

had cost him all the good will he had earned with his poetry: in the eyes of the authorities, at any rate, this poet-prodigy was an *enfant terrible* or even a dangerous radical whose work would bear watching. He had the disconcerting habit, as one of his editors noted, of "thinking aloud the moment an impression strikes him, without reflecting that the whole world is listening to him." It was a habit that nearly landed him in prison but brought him to Paris instead. He was to spend the rest of his life there as a displaced poet, exiled from his public and his mother tongue. Ford Madox Ford, one of the few English writers who have been able to translate Heine's almost untranslatable poetry with most of the cutting edge left intact, understood the deep-rooted ambiguities of his personality. "He is at once romanticist, realist, impressionist, folk-song-folklore German lyricist, French lost soul, Jewish Christian, and the one man who cannot have been descended from the brute beasts."

The intellectual *monde* of Paris in 1831 was more than usually young, ardent, and articulate. The preliminary skirmishes of romanticism had been fought and won: in every sphere of art there was an air of great expectations. Victor Hugo, whose long-haired supporters had routed the clean-shaven followers of classicism at the battle of *Hernani* a year earlier, had just completed his first novel, *Notre Dame de Paris*. Hector Berlioz had just dinned the *Symphonie Fantastique* into Parisian ears as a signal that a revolution was impending in the concert hall. A determinedly independent woman writer, George Sand, had recently made her literary debut in *Le Figaro*. Among the older writers, Stendhal, "the first *modern* man," had just published his masterpiece, *The Red and the Black*. Delacroix was emerging as the most brilliantly gifted of the young painters; Dumas as the most exciting playwright; Balzac, just beginning his *Human Comedy*, as the most panoramic of novelists. Alfred de Musset, Gérard de Nerval, and Alfred de Vigny were experimenting with new forms and rhythms in poetry, much as the two expatriate pianists, Chopin and Liszt, were inventing a new range of images for the keyboard.

A gallery of their portraits—painted by Delacroix, lithographed by Achille Devéria, or engraved by Luigi Calamatta—reveals a series of astonishingly interesting faces. Even allowing for a conventional amount of flattery, these are exceptionally elegant men and beautiful women; sensuous, intelligent, touched by the fire of the romantic imagination. A generation was coming

of age: *"une génération ardente, pâle, nerveuse,"* as Musset wrote. Conceived between two battles, raised to the sound of Napoleonic drums, they now stood poised on the threshold of a new era. "Behind them lay ruins," Musset said, "the fossils of absolutism; before them lay an immense horizon, the dawn of a new age, and between these two points

During his stay in Paris, Heine saw the city's celebrated monuments take shape: the column in the place Vendôme (top); the place de la Concorde, where an obelisk would soon be erected; and the Arc de Triomphe, which was eventually completed in 1836.

Hugo, by Daumier

INFIGHTING: *HERNANI*

Declaring that "romanticism is nothing but liberalism in literature," Victor Hugo took direct aim at the Royalists in his drama *Hernani*. Its première at the Comédie Française on February 25, 1830, right, was characterized by partisan catcalls and cheers, and although the play received mixed notices, the theatre was sold out night after night. Romanticism had clearly won the day.

Hugo's band of eighty young bohemians heckle the Royalist hecklers at the première of Hernani.

an ocean of uncertainty . . . a stormy sea full of shipwrecks."

Heine plunged recklessly into this "maelstrom of events, the waves of the day, the seething revolution." Paris for him was "a pantheon of the living." All the important artists were here: "Paris is not merely the capital of France but of the whole civilized world, the mecca of the intellectual elite. . . . A new art, a new life is being created here, and the creators of this new world lead tumultuously joyful lives." He saw the romantic movement as a constellation of stars of the first magnitude, illuminating the whole of France with the fierce light of its ideas and ideals. "The hearts of great men are the stars of earth; and doubtless when one looks down from above on our planet, these hearts are seen to send forth a silvery light just like the stars of heaven. From such an exalted vantage point, one might perhaps perceive how many radiant stars are scattered over the face of the earth. . . . how radiant with them is France, the Milky Way of great human hearts!"

Equally fascinating was the city of Paris itself, for Heine had always been an incorrigible crowd- and people-watcher. The French writer Philarète Chasles once caught a glimpse of him standing on one of the banks of the Seine during a summer thundershower—"a small, blond man, leaning against the parapet of the quay, holding his dripping hat in one hand, watching the people going past, and the rainstorm." Chasles was fascinated by this stranger with the billowing hair, who seemed to have nothing else to do but look at people. The sun came out again. "His kind and rather moody glance rested on the children and the young married women enjoying the sun; the bootblacks shouting to attract customers. This man had something in his whole manner that was so untroubled and yet so serious; his gaze was so steadfast and yet so quick-moving, that I carried an image of him . . . long after he had disappeared from sight."

*T*he horse-drawn omnibus had been introduced to Paris in 1828, and Heine regarded this as the perfect way to see the sprawling city. When visitors came to see him he would suggest getting on the first bus that passed. "Where is the coachman headed?" "It doesn't matter. We can talk more comfortably here, and later we can choose another." He took aimless rides around the oldest and most disreputable districts, and went slumming with the composer Giacomo Meyerbeer—disguised in workingmen's caps and old jackets—in the dives and cabarets that surrounded Les Halles of the pre-cast-iron epoch.

The sights of Paris were not then confined mainly to monuments and mementos of former glories. "Never has there been so much building going on in Paris as at this moment under the aegis of Louis Philippe," Heine reported in 1833. "Everywhere there are construction sites for new buildings and even whole new streets. The Tuileries and the Louvre reverberate with the sound of constant hammering. The plan for the new Bibliothèque is the most splendid one could imagine. The Church of the Madeleine, formerly the Napoleonic Temple of Fame, is nearing completion. . . . On the place de la Bastille there is a giant elephant, a not unreasonable symbol of the conscious power and intelligence of the people. On the place de la Concorde we can already see a wooden model of the obelisk of Luxor: in a few months the Egyptian original will be erected there, to serve as a memorial to the horrifying events that once took place there [the execution of Louis XVI]."

Nearby, in the galleries of the Louvre, Heine would wander for hours through endless collections of old masters, and the vast array of new paintings exhibited there each year at the official Salon. Af-

Delacroix (center, top hat in hand), graces a salon in this water-color sketch by Eugène Lami.

George Sand, by Musset

SALONS: "A PANTHEON OF THE LIVING"

Heine was welcomed warmly into the salons of Paris, where the best and the brightest artists, musicians, literati, and culture-minded socialites regularly gathered to talk and perform, to see and be seen. Among those present at such soirees were George Sand (provocative behind her fan, above) and her current lover, Alfred de Musset, lounging casually against the fireplace.

terward he remembered that what surprised him most about Paris in 1831 were the pictures he saw in that year's exhibition, notably the great tribute to the July revolution, *Liberty Leading the People,* that Delacroix had painted in a sudden access of patriotic fervor ("If I have won no victories for my country I can at least paint for it") and that had made its debut the very month of Heine's arrival.

Heine's essays on French politics all point to the fact that the work of the French Revolution in bestowing *égalité* on its citizens had been left unfinished, "and today we are still standing on that battlefield." Despite the reassuring presence of the felt hat and furled umbrella of Louis Philippe, the citizen-king and, as Heine said, "the most bourgeois man in France," there were widespread misery and unrest among the poor. France then had a population of some 32 million: as Armand Marrast wrote in the republican *Tribune,* among them were "500,000 sybarites, 1 million happy slaves, but 21 million helots and pariahs, condemned from birth to suffer all the possible tortures of mind and body." Though the old landed noblesse had lost its power, the country was now in the hands of the bankers. The government itself, said Proudhon, had become a *bancocratie.* Heine agreed that power now resided in

the vaults of the Paris Bourse, a great neoclassic temple of finance that had been one of Napoleon's main architectural legacies. "The most beautiful building in Paris," he conceded, adding that he was appalled by what went on inside, on the floor of the exchange, "with its shrill people and its grating sounds, the roar of voices like an ocean of self-interest, with the great bankers surfacing in this human sea like snapping sharks—this is where the interests reside that decide whether there shall be war or peace in our day."

Events in Paris furnished a constant reminder that "the great conflict of our time has not yet been resolved, and the earth still trembles beneath our feet." The class struggle erupted into open warfare again when the republicans took to the barricades in June, 1832. "They were mainly students, handsome youngsters from the Ecole d'Alfort, artists, journalists, in fact all sorts of upward-striving people," Heine explains. They fought in the workers' district around the porte Saint-Martin, within earshot of Heine's flat, and were mowed down by the National Guard, just as Victor Hugo describes the scene in *Les Misérables.* "Here flowed the most ardent blood of France," was Heine's epitaph for the insurrectionists.

But the carnage of the revolt was

overshadowed by a far more general and terrifying disaster that had struck Paris two months earlier—the great cholera epidemic of 1832, which had already decimated the poorer quarters of the city. The cholera had been imported from Calcutta, via London and points east. The first deaths were reported at the end of March; by the end of April almost thirteen thousand were dead from the disease. Heine writes that when the first warnings were posted, everyone refused to believe them and went about their carnival celebrations as usual:

Since the weather was sunny and pleasant, and this was the day of the *demi-carême,* the Parisians poured all the more cheerfully onto the boulevards, where one could even see masks whose multicolored grimaces were supposed to lampoon both the cholera and the widespread fear of the disease. That same evening they attended the carnival balls as always; their gaiety and laughter almost drowned out the loudest music; they grew overheated doing the *chahut,* a dance of not very ambiguous meaning, and swallowed a great deal of sherbet and cold drinks: suddenly the gayest of the harlequins felt a cold draft about the legs and took off his mask, revealing to the astonishment of all present a face that was violet-blue in color. It was soon remarked that this time it was not a joke, and the laughter died on their lips. Several wagons full of people drove from the ball straight to the Hôtel-Dieu, the central hospi-

Alfred de Musset

This illustrious salon—assembled by Mme de Girardin, at center—includes Balzac (left), Delacroix, Liszt, and Sand (grouped around the piano), and Hugo (right). Not present, but sure to be invited on other evenings, were Musset, Berlioz, and Stendhal.

Franz Liszt

Stendhal

Hector Berlioz

tal, where, dressed in their adventurous masks and costumes, they promptly expired. Since, in the initial panic, it was thought they might be infectious, and the regular patients of the Hôtel-Dieu raised such a great cry of fear, these dead people were buried in such haste that, it is said, there was not even time to remove their parti-colored fools' costumes, and they now lie in their graves as happily as they lived.

Though the cholera was no respecter of persons, it had a peculiarly undemocratic way of discriminating against the poor. For reasons not understood by the perplexed physicians of the day, it killed three times as many inhabitants per thousand in the crowded slums than in the fashionable faubourgs. Thinking that the air had something to do with it (it was, of course, spread by sewage and drinking water), the wealthier Parisians decamped en masse. "The people grumbled bitterly when they saw that the rich had fled, and had hied themselves off to healthier regions, attended by doctors and apothecaries," Heine wrote. "With dismay the poor realized that money had now become a talisman against death as well. Most of the *juste milieu* and the great financial world have since departed, and live in their chateaux. But the real representatives of wealth, the Barons de Rothschild, have stayed on in Paris,

demonstrating thereby that it is not only in money matters that they enjoy taking risks. At the same time Casimir Périer [the prime minister] has shown splendid courage in visiting the sick at the Hôtel-Dieu." Périer was to pay for his bravery with his life; he was among scores of eminent cholera victims, ranging from Jean François Champollion, the Egyptologist who had recently solved the riddle of hieroglyphics, to Baron Cuvier, the founding father of comparative anatomy.

The whole of Paris was traumatized by the cholera; it made an unforgettable impression on the young poets and intellectuals, most of whom had never come face to face with death, at least in such frightening form. Louis Blanc, in his *Histoire de dix ans,* writes that the victim turned into a cadaver even before he quitted this life. "His face shriveled up with breathtaking speed: one could count the muscles beneath the skin, which rapidly became blue-black. His eyes sank back into their sockets . . . his breath was cold, his mouth pale and humid, his pulse beat feebly, his words were whispers." George Sand, living on the top floor of Number 25, quai Saint-Michel, held her breath as she saw the cholera creep up the stairs "floor by floor," carrying away six other occupants of the house before "stopping at

the door of our attic, as though it could not deign to be bothered with such insignificant prey."

Dumas actually caught the disease and—displaying the advantages of a bull-like constitution—cured himself by drinking a glassful of ether. Hugo, in his notebooks, castigates the *"pauvres misérables bourgeois égoïstes"* who disregarded the sufferings of the poor during this catastrophe. Gérard de Nerval, who had gone on to medical school despite his early success as a poet, found himself in the front lines of the battle: "I am attending cholera cases, like all students, because of the shortage of physicians," he wrote to a friend. "I assure you it is something terrible."

"A deathly stillness reigns over all Paris," Heine wrote as the epidemic gathered momentum. "A stony expression is on all faces. For several evenings few people have been seen on the boulevards, and what few there were passed each other hurriedly by, with their hands or a cloth in front of their mouths. The theatres are empty. If I go into a salon people are astonished to see me still in Paris, since I have no business to keep me here." He told his friends that he was "too lazy" to leave the city, but the truth does him more credit: with impenetrable sang-froid he was nursing a visiting cousin, brother of the faithless

The duc d'Orléans visits cholera patients at the Hôtel-Dieu, in a painting by Alfred Johannot.

Casimir Pierre Périer

Baron Georges Cuvier

Amalie, who managed to recover from the disease. But when Heine sat down at his writing table, "I was much disturbed in my work by the horrible screams of my neighbor who died of cholera. . . . It is very distracting to have the sound of death sharpening his scythe constantly dinned into one's ear."

After the epidemic had run its course, he wrote:

It was a time of terror, far more terrifying than that earlier time when the executions took place so swiftly and secretly. A masked hangman with an invisible guillotine drove about Paris. "One after the other we are put into the sack," said my servant every morning with a groan as he told me the number of dead or reported the death of a friend. The phrase "put into the sack" was no figure of speech. Coffins soon gave out and the majority of the dead were buried in sacks. . . . [Beside one public market], piled high on top of each other, were many hundreds of white sacks which contained corpses; one could hear very few voices, only those of the gravediggers counting over the sacks for the graves with uncanny indifference, and in muffled tones re-counting them as they loaded their carts with them, or grumbled aloud that they had been given a sack too few, and then not infrequently a strange quarrel would arise. I remember that two little boys stood by me with sad faces and one asked me if I could tell him in which sack his father was.

Heine attended the funeral of a friend and accompanied the hearse to the Père Lachaise cemetery. At the approach to the gates they were brought to a halt by the huge traffic jam.

My coachman stopped, and I, awakening from my reveries, could see literally nothing but sky and coffins. I was among several hundred vehicles bearing the dead, which formed a queue before the narrow gate, and as I could not escape I was obliged to pass several hours amid these gloomy surroundings. Out of ennui, I asked the coachman the name of my neighbor-corpse, and—unhappy coincidence—he named a young lady whose coach had, some months before, as I was going to a ball at Lointier, been crowded against mine and delayed just as it was today. There was only this difference, that then she had often put out of the window her little head, decked with flowers, her lively face lit by the moon, and manifested the most charming vexation and impatience at the delay. Now she was quite still, and perhaps blue. . . .

One may learn at deathbeds how to die, and then await death cheerfully; but to learn to be buried, among the graves of quicklime, of the cholera corpses of Père Lachaise—that is impossible. I hastened to the highest hill of the cemetery, whence one may see the city spread out in all its beauty. The sun was setting—its last rays seemed to bid me a sad farewell; twilight vapors covered Paris with a white shroud, and I wept bitterly over the unhappy city, the city of freedom, of inspira-

tion, and of martyrdom; this savior-city which has already suffered so much for the temporal deliverance of humanity.

Heine had come to Paris only for an extended visit, but the months stretched into years. Asked if he intended to return to Germany, he replied, with his usual ironic smile, that he was "Tannhäuser, trapped in the Venusberg . . . the enchantress won't let me go." The Prussian government then slammed the door behind him by placing both Heine and his works under a sentence of banishment. But although he accepted a yearly stipend from the French privy purse, he refused to become a naturalized French citizen. "The stonecutter who is called upon to adorn my tombstone will find no one to protest when he engraves these words: 'Here lies a German poet.'" Berlioz, undertaking his first concert tour of Germany, wrote an open letter to Heine to tell him that he had not been forgotten at home:

What infinite tenderness breathes through the secret recesses of your heart for the country which you have so often satirized, this land fruitful in poets, this country of dreaming genius—this Germany, in fact, whom you call your old grandmother, and who loves you so well notwithstanding. I could see this in the sadly tender way in which you were spoken of during my journey. Yes, she loves you! On you she has con-

"A DEATHLY STILLNESS"

During Heine's stay in Paris, nothing affected him as greatly as the cholera epidemic of 1832. When the first reports of the disease were posted, Paris was gaily celebrating its pre-Lenten carnival with outlandish costumes and riotous parties. Revelry was soon replaced by tragedy, as the ever-lengthening death lists were published. By the time the epidemic had run its course, thousands had died, including the prime minister, Casimir Périer, and the noted anatomist Baron Cuvier. Those who could afford it fled the city, but Heine stayed on, often accompanying the long processions to Père Lachaise cemetery, where he surveyed his beloved city and wept bitterly over the suffering and death he was witnessing there.

Carnival revelers ride through the streets of Paris in this engraving by an anonymous artist.

centrated all her affections. Your great elder brothers are dead. She now counts only upon you, and . . . calls you her naughty child.

But Heine knew that he would be free to write as he pleased only if he remained in exile. Besides, he was still wholly captivated by Paris and would have exchanged it for no other city. Once, many years after he first came to Paris, he wrote: "I returned here yesterday after a four weeks' absence, and I confess that my heart sang with joy in my breast as the stagecoach rolled over the beloved pavements of the boulevards and I passed the first fashion shop, with its laughing grisette faces—as I heard the tinkle of the cocoa vender's bell and as the blessed gracious air of the city floated toward me."

By that time, to his friends' astonishment, one of these laughing grisettes had become his wife. Mathilde Mirat was nineteen and a shop assistant in her aunt's shoe store when Heine met her in 1834; at the time she could neither read nor write. Heine was delighted that Mathilde knew nothing of poetry and had no inkling that her lover was one of the Great Men of Literature: it gave him the delicious sensation of being loved incognito. "She loves me for myself," he liked to boast, "and my literary reputation has nothing to do with it."

His friends describe her as a dark-haired beauty "of opulent form" who had a radiant smile and a penchant for throwing tantrums. "In a fit of temper she was capable of beating herself with her own fists," recalled the Alsatian writer Alexandre Weill. "Two minutes later her fury would be drowned in tears and sobs. . . . At those times she was not a woman but a child, and like a child she would stamp her foot, hit herself, and fling herself to the ground. . . . It was hilarious."

*H*eine took all this in good grace. "She is absolutely aboriginal and *sui generis*," he insisted, "that is why I love her so much. Despite her bad temper she never harms a fly. She loves animals, especially parrots, and she doesn't read cheap novels." He spent more than ten thousand francs of his hard-earned money to send her to a girls' *pensionnat* where she could learn to read and write, and also acquire some of the social graces. Heinrich Laube accompanied him one Sunday when he went to watch her progress at the school: "The young students had organized a little ball, and we were supposed to watch Heine's 'little woman' as she danced. She was by far the tallest of them all, but to his delight she danced as

gracefully as a young girl, like the most petite debutante."

He had bought her from her aunt for three thousand francs, and in return she was unshakably, even menacingly, devoted to him. "You belong to me!" she would say in a threatening tone of voice. "Wherever you go, I'll go with you, to the end of the world; even to hell itself! I belong to you because you bought me, but I've also bought you—you know the price—and you belong to me for life!" Laube says that they played together like children, and that Heine loved her tenderly in a wholly unliterary fashion. For six years they simply lived together; then Heine married her in what he supposed might be his eleventh hour, on the eve of a pistol duel that he fought in 1841 with one of the many minor literati he had insulted in his essays. (The opponent's bullet merely grazed Heine, and the poet fired into the air.) His subsequent attempts to introduce Mme Heine to polite society were short-lived. After a dinner *chez* Heine to which the journalist Jules Janin and Hector Berlioz were also invited, the poet Léon Gozlan had the effrontery to write in Heine's guest book: *"Il n'y a q'un seul moyen de se défaire d'une vieille maîtresse. Il faut en faire sa femme."* (There is only one way to rid oneself of an old mistress: marry her.).

Heine's health was already causing him a great deal of concern: he had begun his long and terrible descent into the "mattress grave." The first signs of the trouble had appeared as early as 1832, when he complained in a letter that he was unable to move two fingers in his left hand. Gradually the whole left side of his body became paralyzed. In the early 1840's he told one of his women friends, "Now I can only eat on one side, and only cry with one eye! I'm only half a man . . . in the future, will I only be entitled to half your heart?"

For a time he was still able to go limping around Paris, meeting his friends in the cafés and visiting the reading rooms that subscribed to the German newspapers. Mentally, at least, he was unaffected, and he lost none of his presence of mind: once, on a visit to the young revolutionary Karl Marx, recently arrived from Germany with his wife, Jenny, he saved the life of their infant daughter by improvising a cure for the baby's nearly fatal attack of colic. But by the end of the 1840's he was confined to his bed "like Prometheus chained to a rock." Friedrich Engels wrote to Marx that Heine seemed to be "dying piece by piece." Even so he proved to be far tougher than anyone suspected, and his life as a bedridden paralytic dragged on incredibly, year after year.

It was Mathilde who kept him alive, after her own fashion. One night, during one of his periodic crises, when it seemed that his last hour had struck, she rushed to his bedside, took his hand in hers, and cried, "No, Henri, you can't do this to me; you can't die! Just this morning my parrot died, and if you did, too, I'd be too miserable." Heine recovered because, as he said, he had always allowed himself to be swayed by "really cogent reasons." During these last years only a handful of his old friends made the pilgrimage to his bedside. Gérard de Nerval was the great exception: he "visited me every day in my solitude at the barrière de la Santé in order to work quietly with me at the translations of my peaceful German fantasies. . . . Gérard's diction flowed with a lovely and inimi-

Heine, above in a sketch by Charles Gleyre, was bedridden during his later years, and heard only from a distance the thunder of cannon in the Revolution of 1848 (opposite is a battle in the boulevard des Capucines).

table purity, which resembled only the great graciousness of his soul. He was, indeed, more soul than man . . . yet I found in him none of the egoism of the artist; he had a childlike frankness, he had a sensitive delicacy, he was kind and loved all the world."

Gérard, however, was already suffering from intermittent attacks of insanity and was soon to commit suicide. "Whom Jove wants to punish he turns into a poet," Heine told a young writer who had just seen Gérard, at Heine's bedside, go drifting off into incoherence. "This evening you have seen one great poet: he is insane. Come to see me on Thursday and I will show you Alfred de Musset, who seeks forgetfulness and death in a bottle of absinthe, and is certain to find them soon. . . . And look at Heinrich Heine, doctor of jurisprudence, who has a disease of the spinal cord. . . . He too is a poet of our times who will die of a sort of poetic delirium tremens."

Yet the poetry persisted. A special table was made for him so that, propped up on his mattress, he could go on writing with his one "good" hand, with which he could just manage to scrawl poems in inch-high letters. His mattress grave, far from stifling his genius, only deepened and intensified it, and he continued to produce masterpieces: the *Romanzero, Atta Troll* ("the last woodland song of romanticism, and I its last poet"), the poems of protest against the

suppression of the German and Hungarian revolutions, the last love songs, the poems of *Lazarus*. It was as if his beloved Paris had rewarded Heine for his attentions by instilling him with the spirit of François Villon:

How slowly time, the frightful snail,
Crawls to the corner that I lie in;
While I, who cannot move at all,
Watch from the place that I must die in.

His brother Gustav, who came to pay his last respects, realized with a shock that "this was a whole new world, which he had created for himself on this bed of pain." Yet at the same time he still kept up with Paris—but from a distance, the way he heard the thunder of cannon during the Revolution of 1848. In his last apartment, on the top floor of a house on the avenue Matignon, near the Champs Elysées, all of his windows looked out over the city; he had a tent made on a balcony, surrounded by flowerpots, so that with his one remaining eye he could take a last panoramic look at this Paris he had loved so well. It was the Louvre he missed most of all. "Imagine," he told one of his friends, "a man like me, who loves art so much, has not seen a painting in seven years!"

He wanted the Parisians to remember him as he had been when he still moved about the city like a fish in the sea, *"moi qui suis presque français dans mes idées et dans la vie"* (I who am almost French in my ideas and in life). When the *Revue des deux mondes* published a picture of him "with bowed head like a painting of Christ by Morales," he complained to Théophile Gautier that this had "caused these good people to feel much too sorry for me," and asked him to "place my former picture in place of this tragic mask." He was determined to the end to see the world through the rose-colored screen of Parisian gaiety. He died in 1856, probably more thoroughly prepared for the event than any other poet before or since. Just before his death he said to Mathilde, who was praying fervently at his bedside: "Calm yourself, my child, God will forgive me; after all, it's his métier!"

STAVISKY
and the Fall of France

In Alain Resnais's recent, brilliant film, the dealings of
a high-placed swindler bring down the Third Republic. But
who was the real Stavisky, and how wide was his reach?

With the exception of the monarchy, the Third Republic was the longest-lasting regime ever to govern France. Between its difficult birth in 1870 and its unlamented death in 1940, it managed to endure for seventy years. It led France to victory in World War I and produced leaders like Clemenceau. It presided for a time over the most powerful nation in Europe, a prosperous nation with a great empire and an enlightened civilization. But in the midst of these achievements something happened to the Third Republic that sapped its vitality, and at the first sign of an external threat it rolled over and expired. The collapse was sudden but its roots were deep: the Third Republic was suffering from a steady, creeping enfeeblement for which there was no cure. As Livy said about the decline of Rome, it could endure neither its vices nor their remedies.

Among the vices, there was the instability of revolving-door governments, 107 in all, or an average of one and a half per annum. There was a clan of recurring mediocrities like Aristide Briand and Edouard Daladier at the helm, and the multiparty system contributed to the vacuum of authority. Then, too, the nation was increasingly polarized between a disillusioned left and a right that admired fascism. There was also a population drain (France's postwar population was 39 million, compared with 63 million for Germany), caused by a zero growth rate and the death of a million and a half people in World War I.

Jean-Paul Belmondo, left, portrayed Serge Alexandre Stavisky with jaunty amorality in Alain Resnais's 1975 film. The real Stavisky, at right, was photographed shortly before his suicide in early 1934.

The trauma of that four-year blood bath had made France numerically and psychologically unfit to fight another war twenty years later. Among the people there was a widespread attitude of cynicism and defeatism (*je m'en foutisme*), while the sclerotic high command, obsessed with the idea of a continuous defensive front, argued that the horse was better than the tank and that there could be no such thing as aerial combat. There was the flight of capital, a devalued franc, a backward industry, a venal and irresponsible press, and a bankrupt "peace at any price" foreign policy. Finally, there was a series of financial scandals that further undermined the regime by pointing to corruption in high places. Foremost among these was the Stavisky scandal, which was rather more sweeping than the others since members of all three branches of government were involved. Thanks to Stavisky, the government fell, and Paris experienced the worst street riots it had seen in sixty years.

Perhaps it was the idea of the shabby con man as giant killer that appealed to the gifted film maker Alain Resnais. Perhaps it was the analogy with our own time, in which Stavisky could be seen as the key figure in a decaying system that provides a congenial environment for parasites that eventually destroy it.

In this sense his film *Stavisky* is fascinating. It is faithful to the style of the period and generally careful in its presentation of the facts. Stavisky, played by Jean-Paul Belmondo with just the right tone of jaunty amorality, is seen as a sort of French Arturo Ui, who rises in the system and is accepted by the establishment precisely because he is unprincipled. The Third Republic, Resnais is telling us, was a period when dishonesty was rewarded. He is also telling us that there are hierarchies of dishonesty. There is, first, Stavisky the petty crook who prospers thanks to his government connections. There is also the system, which closes ranks when it is threatened by Stavisky and arranges for his disappearance. And there is, finally, the reaction of an enraged public opinion, fanned by a dishonest press, which uses Stavisky as a way of bringing down the system.

Stavisky is a brilliant entertainment, but in making its point dramatically, the film becomes disconnected from history. Perhaps this is true of most theatre of fact, even the greatest examples, like Shakespeare's *Richard III*. If it succeeds as theatre, it fails as history. *Stavisky* the film suffers from the single-cause fallacy. To say that Stavisky the man was

By TED MORGAN

the agent of the Third Republic's demise is like saying that the *ancien régime* came to an end because of the Freemasons or the high price of bread. To isolate one piece from the mosaic of decline and make it serve as a total explanation makes a better story but wanders quite a long way from the truth. Seen off camera, the Stavisky case was not the Third Republic's coffin, it was really only one of the nails in the coffin, and a fairly blunt one at that. Other scandals had already established in the public mind the connection between government officials and crooked business deals. In 1928, for instance, Clemenceau's minister of justice and one of the signers of the Versailles treaty, a man named Louis-Lucien Klotz, was arrested for passing bad checks. In 1930 a shady bank run by a man named Oustric failed despite his influence in high places.

When the Stavisky case broke in 1933, the world depression had reached France. Unemployment was high, the franc was weak, and civil servants had just taken a 6 per cent pay cut. A great many citizens—among them the civil servants with amputated salaries, the petty bourgeoisie by necessity dipping into their savings, and the *rentiers* whose fixed incomes had dropped 20 per cent because of devaluation—were in a belligerent mood.

It was against this backdrop of discontent and lack of confidence in elected officials that Sacha Stavisky took stage center. He did not look like Jean-Paul Belmondo. He was short and stoop-shouldered and had sleepy eyes, a pinched mouth, and a toothbrush mustache. He came from a decent middle-class background. He did not become a criminal because of a deprived childhood or bad companions, but by vocation. He belonged to a species that finds its greatest satisfaction in duping others, a species that Jung, in *Archetypes and the Collective Unconscious*, calls the trickster-figure, whose aim is to master the world through guile,

just as the engineer masters it through mathematics and technology. The trickster-figure appears in every age: in eighteenth-century Italy his name was Scapino, and in the France of the 1930's his name was Stavisky.

While still in his teens, Stavisky started passing bad checks and counterfeiting treasury bills. In his twenties, he was arrested for adding an extra zero to a four-thousand-franc check. In 1926, charged with swindling two stockbrokers out of seven million francs, he was again arrested, in the middle of a dinner party in a luxurious villa in Marly-le-Roi, in the presence of his pretty mistress, Arlette Simon, whom he later married. The scandal was too much for his father, who killed himself. Stavisky spent eighteen months in jail before being released to await a trial that never came. By that time he had turned police informer, receiving favors in exchange. Between 1926 and 1934 his trial was adjourned nineteen times. Stavisky, who had changed his name to Serge Alexandre, seemed to be above the law. It did not improve matters that the head of the Paris Parquet (the public prosecutor's office responsible for the delays), Georges Pressard, was Premier Camille Chautemps's brother-in-law; or that the man who did the actual postponing, Albert Prince, was later found on the rails of the Paris-Dijon line, probably murdered.

As Stavisky's influence grew, he began to paint on a larger canvas. Why

swindle a man with a forged check when you could swindle an entire city, an entire country? He bought a theatre and interests in newspapers. He was seen in the company of cabinet ministers. He hired four members of the Chamber of Deputies as lawyers. (It was one of the worst failings of the Third Republic that a lawyer who was elected to the Chamber could continue to practice in civil and criminal cases.)

It was in 1928 that Stavisky launched his first national swindle. Every French city has a government-licensed pawnshop, or Crédit Municipal, where citizens in need of cash can hock their jewelry. Stavisky had himself named as the agent to float a bond issue backed by the Crédit Municipal of Orléans. He used fake emeralds as collateral for the bonds, which he discounted at a legitimate bank, using the money to fund new ventures. In one year he made off with ten million francs' worth of bonds. Using money obtained from another swindle, he was able to redeem them before he was caught.

In 1930 he moved the Crédit Municipal operation to Bayonne, a sleepy city of thirty thousand near the Spanish border. He had somehow obtained from the minister of labor, Albert Dalimier, two letters endorsing the Bayonne bonds. Stavisky promptly floated twice as many bonds as were covered by deposits, a total of 239 million francs' worth. Two sets of books were used to conceal the discrepancy. No one found it suspicious that a town of modest size should float such a large bond issue—one explanation given was the influx of Spanish refugees. With Dalimier's endorsement, Stavisky sold the bonds to insurance companies, who were under the impression that they were guaranteed by the state.

Stavisky had no way of redeeming the bonds until he launched an even bigger swindle. He discovered some obscure bonds that had been issued in accordance with the Treaty of Trianon to benefit

In the film, Anny Duperey, left, played the role of Stavisky's mistress and wife, Arlette Simon. In true life, Arlette was a former Chanel model. In the 1930's, right, she posed dripping with ermine.

The mayor of Bayonne, Joseph Garat, left, was a participant in Stavisky's swindle, in which bonds like the one at right were redeemed on phony credit.

Stavisky spent large sums on jewels, some of which are above. When he was strapped for cash he pawned them, at least once at the London shop at right.

Early in January, 1934, Stavisky was found dead by the police, who claimed he had committed suicide, in a locked room in this Alpine villa at Chamonix.

Later, his body was returned to Paris for an autopsy. Investigators upheld the verdict of suicide but reproached the police for their unorthodox methods.

Hungarians living on Rumanian territory who wished to be repatriated. During the postwar years, the bonds had gradually gone the way of other reparation payments, losing most of their value. Stavisky bought up these Hungarian bonds for a fraction of their nominal value, and in the summer of 1933 went to see the minister of labor (no longer the same one who had endorsed the Bayonne bonds) and announced that he had found a way to abolish unemployment. Naturally the minister was interested, since unemployment was his biggest headache. Stavisky's plan was to found a company that would lend money to local authorities at low interest rates to launch public works projects. The money would be raised by floating bonds. The bonds would be guaranteed by his Hungarian bonds.

The minister of labor was sufficiently impressed to ask the Ministry of Finance for an opinion. The opinion came —it was unfavorable. The Ministry of Finance went further. It published a circular warning prospective buyers against the phony bonds. The irony here is that although Stavisky had been helped by friends in high places, he was finally destroyed because the government was not dishonest enough.

The Finance Ministry circular was the start of his ruin. In December, 1933, when tax inspectors took a close look at the books of the Bayonne Crédit Municipal, the first mention of the scandal appeared in the press. Several arrests were made in Bayonne, and Stavisky was persuaded to disappear. He obtained a false passport, and left Paris to hibernate in the Alpine ski resort of Chamonix.

With Stavisky's disappearance, the right-wing press seized on the affair to attack the Chautemps government. The Royalist *Action Française* led the way with violent editorials denouncing corruption, and published the two Dalimier letters. A cartoon in the *Echo de Paris* showed Dalimier at dinner, looking despondently into the sauceboat and saying: "The Bayonnaise has turned." Thanks to daily revelations hinting at far-reaching corruption, the scandal gathered momentum. On January 7, 1934, the *Action Française* ran a banner headline saying "Down with the Thieves" and called for street demonstrations.

On January 8, the police located Stavisky's Chamonix villa and forced the door to his room. The police said they found him stretched out at the foot of his bed in a skiing outfit, and that he had shot himself in the temple. No one in Paris believed this version. In rare agreement, the Communist *Humanité* and the Royalist *Action Française* concluded that Stavisky had been murdered because he knew too much. The classic headline which Resnais used in his film, was: *"Stavisky s'est suicidé d'une balle qui lui a été tirée à bout portant."* (Stavisky committed suicide with a bullet that was fired at him pointblank.)

In the film, Stavisky decides at Chamonix to go back to Paris to confront his accusers. It is then that he sees the police arriving and locks himself in his room. The implication is that suicide would have been out of character. A man as dynamic as Stavisky would not have gone down without a fight. The viewer is left with the uneasy feeling that Stavisky's suicide was assisted. In fact, nothing in the historical record gives us any insight into Stavisky's intentions at Chamonix. The parliamentary inquiry that followed his death, which was generally praised for its thoroughness, concluded that Stavisky had killed himself, but blamed the police for their clumsy handling of the operation and said that he could have been taken alive.

The point of Resnais's film is that Stavisky's suspicious death brought about the death of the Third Republic. To sustain this point of view, Resnais has to create a fictional character, the baron Raoul, who is both Stavisky's friend and the emblem of the declining society that Stavisky finishes off. Acted by Charles Boyer with a fine balance of ingenuousness and disenchantment, the baron Raoul is a passive, nostalgic idler who has dissipated his family fortune in pursuit of gentlemanly pleasures. He is conservative but incapable of resisting change. He believes in an aristocracy of like-minded men of honor, but becomes the dupe of the *arriviste* Stavisky.

Throughout the film, the baron Raoul is shown in counterpoint to Stavisky. He wears the rosette of the Legion of Honor in his lapel, for instance, while Stavisky wears a red carnation. In one scene, they are watching auditions for a play Stavisky is producing. A young actress has picked the scene with the Specter from Jean Giraudoux's *Intermezzo*, and

Stavisky volunteers to read the Specter's lines, which are ruminations about death. The implication is clear—the actress represents the Republic, and Stavisky is the messenger of death. Later, at the inquest that follows Stavisky's suicide, the baron testifies that he had no idea that Stavisky was a crook, and repeats, like a visitor from another century, Talleyrand's celebrated remark about the pre-1789 *ancien régime*: he who did not know

France during that time has not known the sweetness of life.

To reinforce his thesis, Resnais introduces another character in the person of Trotsky, who was, in fact, given asylum in France between 1933 and 1935. We glimpse Trotsky on half a dozen occasions in the various abodes of his exile, attracting a following of young people and foreign sympathizers. He and Stavisky never meet, but in Resnais's contrapuntal technique they are

Albert Prince, the judge who had postponed Stavisky's trial on a 1926 swindling charge, was found dead, probably murdered, on the tracks at right.

In November, 1935, Arlette and nineteen others, above, none of them politically important, were tried in Paris for complicity in Stavisky's swindles.

Arlette, above with her attorney, was found not guilty in January, 1936. High government officials, rumored to also be involved, were never brought to trial.

linked, leaving the viewer to ponder the reason for the connection.

The reason is this: Stavisky, like Trotsky, was a Russian Jew, the son of a Kiev dentist who migrated to France in 1900, when Sacha was fourteen. Both were outsiders, one in exile, and the other a naturalized Frenchman, during a period of open anti-Semitism. And both were subversives. Trotsky had helped bring down the *ancien régime* in Russia as Stavisky was now bringing down the remains of the *ancien régime* in France, the one as a revolutionary and the other as a swindler. Resnais pushes the connection further by blaming Trotsky's expulsion on the Stavisky case. The film's argument is as follows: the Stavisky scandal led to a bloody right-wing uprising in the place de la Concorde, which provoked the collapse of the government; the right-wing press charged that granting Trotsky asylum was one of the crimes of a rotten regime, and clamored for his banishment; therefore, afraid of renewed rioting, the government expelled Trotsky. The historical record does not bear out this interpretation. It was not until May, 1935, after Foreign Minister Pierre Laval had gone to Moscow to negotiate a Franco-Soviet alliance with Stalin, that Trotsky, fearing he would be deported, sought refuge in Norway.

History is too untidy to be faithfully adapted to a dramatic form for the stage or the screen. The real drama, as it was played out after Stavisky's death, began with a two-day debate in the Chamber of Deputies on January 11 and 12. In the crowded lobbies, people chanted, "Sta-vis-ky, Sta-vis-ky," like keeners at an Irish wake. The most sensible remark, amid a flood of partisan oratory, was probably made by the Socialist deputy Léo Lagrange, who asked himself how Stavisky had been able to get as far as he did, and answered, "It is simply because he found in our principal social organisms—in the police, in the judiciary, in public and private offices, in the press and in Parliament—a sufficient number of greedy people and a sufficient amount of carelessness and corruption."

Premier Chautemps misjudged the political climate. Perhaps because several of his relatives were implicated (in addition to his brother-in-law Georges Pressard, his brother Pierre was a lawyer for one of Stavisky's companies), he rejected a proposal for a parliamentary inquiry, and became known as the *grand étouffeur*, the great husher-upper.

By this time, there were daily riots in the streets, and fistfights in the Chamber of Deputies. The inflammatory mood was fanned by articles in the *Action Française*, whose circulation, thanks to Stavisky, had soared to half a million. The minister of justice resigned in a minor scandal unrelated to the Stavisky affair, and on January 27, the Chautemps government handed in its resignation. It was the first time in the sixty-four-year history of the Third Republic that a government with a solid majority had been brought down.

Edouard Daladier formed a government, but was no less heavy-handed than his predecessor. He dismissed the director of the Comédie Française, Emile Fabre, whose revival of *Coriolanus* had given rise to demonstrations. Each evening a Royalist claque applauded lines that could only be interpreted as an attack on parliamentary government, such as: "What should the people do with these bald tribunes . . . throw their power in the dust!" Fabre was replaced by M. Thomé, the former head of the Sûreté, who was under a cloud for helping Stavisky. Daladier also dismissed the Paris prefect of police, Jean Chiappe, whose right-wing sympathies were common knowledge. Chiappe was a popular and lively Corsican, whose enduring monument is the *passage clouté*, a pedestrian crossing between two rows of metal studs set in the pavement.

Chiappe's dismissal ignited another series of editorials and calls to take to the streets. He replaced Stavisky as a rallying cry. Stavisky had been the target of the right, and Chiappe became the martyr of the right.

On February 6, 1934, the Daladier government was making its inaugural appearance. Every right-wing group, from the Action Française to the Croix de Feu, told its followers to take to the streets on that day and march on the Chamber of Deputies. The result was the bloodiest uprising since the 1871 Commune. To keep them from overrunning the Chamber, the police fired on the demonstrators. Fourteen rioters and one policeman were killed in the seven-hour battle, and more than two thousand were injured. Among the forty thousand demonstrators were the armed militants of right-wing groups, fascist sympathizers, misguided Communists, and many Parisians who had come out to protest against *les voleurs*, which meant Stavisky and his cronies.

Had the rioters reached the Chamber, it is conceivable that right-wing leaders like Charles Maurras and Colonel François de la Rocque could have taken power and led some sort of fascist regime, and it would be possible to say that the Stavisky case had caused the collapse of the Third Republic. But that did not happen. The Daladier government, less than two weeks old, fell, and was replaced by a government headed by Gaston Doumergue. The Republic was feeble, but it was resilient. It would totter along for another six years. On February 12, in response to the right-wing demonstrations of the previous week, the leftists called a general strike. Communists and Socialists marched together in the place de la République. It was a preview of the Popular Front, the left-wing government that would come to power in 1936.

The Doumergue government, according to one of its critics, was like a poultice on a gangrenous leg. At least Doumergue had the good sense, on February 24, to form two committees of inquiry, one on Stavisky, known as the "thieves' committee," and one on the riots, known as the "murderers' committee." The merit of the "thieves' committee" was that the deputies who made it up did not shrink at implicating their colleagues. Seventeen deputies, the committee found, had been to varying degrees involved with Stavisky. Most heavily involved, of course, were the four he had hired as lawyers. Other high officials were named. A Paris magistrate, dismissed because of his dealings with Stavisky, tried to poison himself. A department head in the Ministry of Agriculture, who had been on the board of directors of one of Stavisky's companies, was dismissed and cut his throat.

Such extremes of remorse were rare, however. The committee did not find a general pattern of corruption. It was, after all, thanks to the vigilance of the Ministry of Finance that Stavisky had been caught. But it did describe a number of ways that public services facilitated corruption. Because he was a police informer, the Sûreté did not look too closely at Stavisky's activities. Because he hired influential lawyers, he was able to obtain trial postponements. Because he said *tu* to deputies and *cher ami* to cabinet ministers, his fraudulent schemes had a veneer of credibility. Because several newspapers were on his payroll, the press ignored him.

Stavisky had a gift for exploiting the favoritism, vanity, and nepotism of the République des Camarades (Republic of Chums). Sometimes there was outright dishonesty, but more often there was carelessness, the muddle of dossiers, an accepted tradition in government departments of putting things off and exchanging favors, and a penchant for negotiated solutions. Stavisky had merely taken advantage of what Edmund Burke called "the confused and scuffling bustle of local agency."

That is why, for all its shortcomings, it would be misleading to describe the Third Republic as corrupt. Once its illness was diagnosed, it had enough antibodies to survive the tumor. Stavisky was less important for what he did than for the way he was used by the opposition. For the Stavisky case brought out something far more serious than influence-peddling, and that was a crisis of authority. As a result of press campaigns and street agitation, two governments, supported by a majority in a democratically elected parliament, were forced to resign. A weak executive, not

Resnais, in his film, draws a parallel between Trotsky, left, who helped bring down the ancien régime *in Russia, and Stavisky, whose swindles caused daily rioting in Paris, right, that contributed to the downfall of the government. There is, however, no reason to believe that Trotsky and Stavisky ever met.*

The film Stavisky *suggests that the scandal ultimately brought about the collapse of the Third Republic. Above, two top leaders of the new Vichy regime, Pierre Laval, the chief of government, and Marshal Pétain, the chief of state, inspect an honor guard of French troops on November 1, 1942.*

corruption, was the Third Republic's mortal sin. The Stavisky scandal gave the right wing the chance to show that it could bring down governments by taking to the streets. Two years later, when the Popular Front came to power, the workers occupied factories in another example of power through mass pressure. Instead of government by ballot box and parliament, there was government by strikes and riots.

When the end came, it was not because of a domestic crisis, but because of an invasion. The enfeebled Republic was unable to fight. With the Germans sweeping through France, the deputies met for the last time in Vichy in July, 1940, and voted to change the constitution, which in effect put an end to the Third Republic. The National Assembly vote was 569 for, 80 against, and 17 abstaining. Senator Boivin-Champeaux, the chairman of the committee

charged with reforming the constitution, pronounced a suitable epitaph: "It is not without sadness that we shall bid adieu to the constitution of 1875. It made France a free country. . . . It died less from its imperfections than from the fault of men who were charged with guarding it and making it work." Proclaimed in 1870 after the French defeat by Prussia, the Third Republic was laid to rest in 1940 as the result of another French defeat. Power was handed over to Marshal Pétain, who at the age of eighty-five was fifteen years older than the Republic he had buried. If any single person should be held responsible for the collapse of the Third Republic, that person is not Stavisky, but Adolf Hitler.

Ted Morgan is a journalist with a long-standing interest in the history of the French, particularly the Third Republic.

THE STRANGEST GARDEN IN THE WEST

Although it is called Bomarzo's Gate of Hell, the monstrous mask opposite is actually the entrance to a cave, above, which is furnished with a stone picnic table that seats six.

Four hundred years ago

a reclusive Italian duke created his own

enchanted forest at Bomarzo.

Here is a guide to its bizarre delights

By ROBERT HUGHES

Built about 1570, the Villa Lante has a show-place Renaissance garden.

Young Man in His Study, *by Lotto, circa 1527*

Mystery surrounds the life of Pierfrancesco Orsini, creator of Bomarzo. No one even knows what he looked like, although a novel about his life has it that Orsini sat for the portrait above by Lorenzo Lotto. At the time he conceived his Sacred Wood, opposite, with its sculptures set in disarray over a hundred acres, the fashion in gardens dictated parterres in symmetrical patterns, like those of the nearby Villa Lante, at left.

The garden lies tangled in its vegetation. Its sculptures, carved out of the cheesy, mica-flecked tufa of the Bomarzo Valley some forty miles north of Rome, have taken four centuries to lose most of their erotic languor or expressive strain, and now—pitted and listing sideways in the gluey clay, patched by gray and green mosses—they have returned to the primitive condition of rocks, outcrops of immobile Etruscan stone whose roots go deep into the ground, sharing its darkness with the forgotten tombs of an earlier people. Some years ago, before the local mayor decided to harness the citizenry to clean up their tourist attraction, one entered by a rusty gate, through whose iron whorls nothing appeared except dark clumps of oaks and a small stone temple with portico and dome that might (or might not) have been designed by Giacomo da Vignola in the sixteenth century. This rational little structure announced a descent, past the triple-headed Cerberus baying beside the broken flight of steps, along a terrace lined with the fallen bomblike hulks of stone acorns, each six feet high, to a colossal nymph. Her skirt often held a pool of rainwater, and her head wore an immense dish in which a clump of

flowering agaves grew. The visitor passed barely decipherable inscriptions on every rock, the rampant bear of the Orsini emblem, and a twin-tailed siren.

Then, below, the second terrace, and an elephant crushing a Roman soldier in its trunk, watched by a silently roaring mask cut into the rock of the hill: you could walk through its stone mouth, beneath the inscription *Ogni pensiero vola* (All thought flies away) cut in the upper lip, and recline on its tongue. A dragon reared up, its wings spotted with Islamic crescents, battling against two mastiffs. Fountains, long since dried and their pipes blocked; a nymphaeum; a leaning tower, but built leaning, and with the fireplaces in its exiguous rooms plumbed straight by whimsical masons —so the path downward into the Sacred Wood continued, along washed-out tracks, under tottering retaining walls that bulged outward under the shifting earth of the valley, past two colossi locked in their endless upside-down murder, and to a thirty-foot-long tortoise and the monstrous mouth of a whale that emerged from the ground beneath it. Bomarzo in late autumn was a peculiarly silent place. No streams, only the seep and drip of water punctuated by occasional birdcalls; it was haunted, but by what chilly afternoon ghost?

This is the strangest garden in the West. Inevitably it is a subject of legends. At dawn, just before the sun rises over the valley, the statue of a woman riding the giant tortoise turns around on her pedestal, once. At midnight on a certain date in March, if you have the courage to wait on the steps that ascend to the *bocca d'inferno*—as the Bomarzese call the mask—its lips will writhe and speak, revealing the time and place of your death. Fairies and worse are reputed to infest the Sacred Wood, and this is attested by one of the inscriptions carved near a fountain: "By night and by day, we watch and are ready to guard this spring against all injury." But if the stories are put aside, and the stone monsters of Bomarzo, together with their layout and inscriptions, are seen as a work of art—that is, as a group of images intended to convey some meaning, however private, esoteric, or otherwise inaccessible—what can be said about this place?

At first not very much, except that Bomarzo is in absolute contrast to the general trend of late Renaissance garden design. In the exquisite grounds of the Villa Lante, built a few miles away near Viterbo for the Gambara cardinals, the pattern is organized around a central axis, a spine of water. Water issues from

Among Bomarzo's marvels are an embattled dragon, an elephant, and a tower that leans toward a hill.

a spring at the top of the hill, descends through a sequence of transformations: down a *chasse d'eau*, out of pools, into fountains, through the trough of a formal banqueting table, underground, and out again to burst with ravishing élan from a star supported by four bronze Moors. With similar formality, you follow its course downhill, through terraces and parterres and flights of steps, all symmetrically arranged. Bomarzo lacks this order and pairing. Instead, the visitor wanders from one "marvel" to the next: the figures and monsters go by like allegorical figures in an elaborate sixteenth-century court masque, except that it is the spectator who moves and not the stone protagonists. The landscaping, the downward path, the sudden apparition of a sculpture at a bend or from an odd angle— these build up a constant level of surprise and must always have done so, even when the carvings were new and the shrubbery less rank. The shock of the images replaces the more common and oafish shocks of Renaissance *giochi d'acqua*, the hidden waterspouts with which Tivoli and the Villa Lante were booby-trapped. In short, Bomarzo even in ruin is a quintessentially Mannerist work of art, informed by the same kind of bizarre and erudite taste for artificial

nature that swept the courts of Europe in the late sixteenth century.*

Very little has been discovered about the man who built Bomarzo. This is odd, for he belonged to one of the most powerful and richly documented families in the history of Renaissance Italy. Pierfrancesco Orsini, duke of Montenero, Collepiccolo, and Castelvecchio, was born sometime between 1512 and 1520; he died in 1585. This country nobleman preferred to all his titles the nickname "Vicino" (the neighbor). He sprang from a notably ruthless line of robber barons who had emerged from the muddled and barbaric squabbles of a collapsed Rome in the tenth century and become one of the supreme clans of the peninsula. (The name Orsini began in the legend that their first ancestor had been suckled by an *orsa*, or she-bear, as Romulus and Remus, the founders of Rome, had been by a wolf bitch.) Vicino's father, a condottiere named Gian Corrado Orsini, acquired Bomarzo in 1502 and, since the site had some strategic value by virtue of its view of the Tiber Valley, converted an existing fortress into the four-hundred-room castle that stands today, jammed into the cliff like a yellow labyrinthine tooth in its petrified gum.

If his son Vicino ever took part in the

*See "Mannerism," HORIZON, Summer, 1973.

rapacious political life of the Orsinis, no record of it survives. Not only are we unaware of what he did, except build a garden; there is also no trace of what he looked like. An Argentinian novelist, Manuel Mujica-Lainez, wrote an opulent fiction (*Bomarzo*, Simon & Schuster, 1969) to flesh out this wraith of Italian history and suggested that the *Young Man in His Study* by Lorenzo Lotto was in fact Vicino. Perhaps so, perhaps not. A local tale has it that Vicino was a hunchback who created a garden of monsters in order to persuade his wife, Julia Farnese, that deformity held its own mysterious principles of delight. But again, there is no evidence for or against the story. Contemporary records of Vicino are quite schematic. As befitted a wealthy duke, he is known to have had a modest court circle of artists and writers and to have written verse himself. One versifier named Betussi praised his genius and his "immense, almost fatal physical beauty." The author-historian Francesco Sansovino also wrote that Vicino was a man "of honorable presence and kingly aspect, who loved not only arms but letters, in which he showed facility and a fertile imagination." All this has an odor of obsequiousness. Court writing, especially in sixteenth-century Italy, was not

reportage and became even less so in proportion to the remoteness and absolutism of the court. Bomarzo was very remote indeed. A poet who failed to discern in his patron the temper of Achilles, the literacy of Virgil, the beauty of Apollo, and the subtlety of Hermes might soon be out of a job.

One of the inscriptions in the garden reads *Vicino Orsini Fec. MDLII*, so the Sacred Wood must have been started at least by 1552. Its construction was to ramble on for another thirty years, and, as is the nature of open-ended and obsessive projects, the park never was finished; the valley of Bomarzo is still strewn with boulders marked by a few preliminary chiselings. Apparently Vicino was still absorbed in it in 1564. A letter from Annibale Caro dated October 20 of that year begs the duke's pardon for not writing earlier; Caro had been as much tied up with his little vineyard at Frascati as the duke was with his "theatres and mausoleums" at Bomarzo. (Clearly the masquelike character of the garden was not lost on Caro.)

By 1580 Vicino confessed in a letter that he was bored with the whole project. He was in his sixties by then, and no more work was done. One may assume that since he had dictated the whole program of the Sacred Wood and even seems to have written its inscriptions, there must have been no reason to continue. In 1645 the duke's property was sold to the della Rovere family, and the gardens began to decay. In the end the *meraviglie*, or marvels, of Vicino Orsini's fantasy went unnoticed for more than three centuries, and not even Goethe, who went into such raptures over the rather less convulsive parade of carved freaks at the Villa Palagonia in Sicily, heard about Bomarzo.

The surrealists rediscovered it. Salvador Dali went there with a squad of *paparazzi* in the 1940's and tried, unsuccessfully, to buy two of the statues for his house in Cadaqués. Bomarzo thus sidled into the surrealist canon, and ever since then, most of the writing about it has been done by critics whose reaction to romantic spots and out-of-the-way

Lion fighting dragon, by Leonardo da Vinci

Poliphilo fleeing dragon, artist unknown

The dragon holding two mastiffs at bay, opposite, echoes two earlier art works, a drawing by Leonardo (top) and a woodcut (above) from a popular allegory of the time, the Hypnerotomachia Poliphili *(Love, Dream, and Battle of Poliphilo), published in 1499.*

ruins was steeped in surrealist ideas of fantasy and enigma. The only book on Bomarzo (other than Mujica-Lainez's novel) was written in 1957 by André Pieyre de Mandiargues, a French novelist, critic, and pornographer. He declared in true surrealist vein that beauty often presents itself in the guise of a nightmare, and

quite unconsciously as a rule, though sometimes quite intentionally, the makers of monuments achieve their greatest splendor when they venture as far as possible from what is taught in the art academies. Thus, in disorder, helped by the forces of nature, some places have been created by human hands which truly possess a mad beauty. I do not know one such place in Europe which contains this last attribute in greater measure than the valley of Bomarzo.

A German critic, Gustav Hocke, took much the same view of Bomarzo in 1957 in a book written expressly to show that sixteenth-century Mannerism and twentieth-century surrealism were manifestations of the same impulse:

Bomarzo is the realization of an "idea" of

nature in which beauty is fused with horror. . . . The deformation of the human body, of architecture; the violence done to nature and even to cosmogony; here, these are the servants of calculated aberration, used consciously as an aesthetic means. Beauty had to be . . . terrorizing, diabolically shocking.

The trouble with this rhetoric is that it has very little to do with the intentions of Vicino Orsini, and even less with the artistic climate of the century in which the garden and its sculptures were made. Whatever else he might have been, Vicino was not a madman, afflicted with melancholia. *Anima quiescens silentior fit* (The soul grows more silent as it is calmed): so reads a cartouche on Vicino's leaning tower. And the theme of the garden as a place of rest, of release, runs through other inscriptions: *Sol per sfogar il cor* (Only to unburden the heart). Is it likely that Vicino would have had such sentiments cut into the rocks of his park if he had meant the place to reduce him and his guests to a terrified pulp of emotion?

In fact, the enigmas of Bomarzo are impervious to a surrealist theory of art, but they may surrender themselves to more orderly tools. Consider what de Mandiargues says about the giant tortoise, surmounted by its draped figure:

On its shell, a bizarre pedestal supports a ball, and on top of this maliciously [*sic*] balanced, stands a statue of a nymph . . . whose hands make the gesture of holding a trumpet. It is likely . . . that this trumpet once existed, and that it produced, by means of the play of water, a music which could only have been celestial or terrifying.

Perhaps there was water music at Bomarzo (another marvel of the sixteenth-century garden designer's skill, the Organ Fountain in the Tivoli Gardens, was roughly contemporary with Bomarzo). But wherever its wheezings and hootings may have issued from, it cannot have been this statue, for there is no hole in the nymph's eroded face through which air could have been blown into the lost trumpet. This figure, balanced on a sphere, her drapery billowing as if in a head wind, is actually

That good luck is slow in coming may be the message of this tortoise carrying Fortuna.

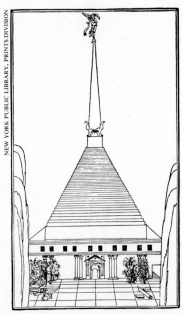

Temple, Hypnerotomachia Poliphili

a common Renaissance allegory. She is Lady Luck, or Fortuna. One of her classical attributes is her swiftness: she flits by, and if you want to seize her, she must be caught by the forelock; you cannot catch up with her. Herein lies the point of the sculpture. It is an elaborate stone joke. Vicino Orsini's *Fortuna* is mounted on a tortoise, the most lethargic of steeds. Her trumpet is the instrument of Fame, which, the *concetto* proclaims, comes too slowly to Vicino, a poet whose works were published only on his ancestral boulders.

Such twists, puns, and literary elaborations are typical of Mannerist court art. They were aimed at members of a sophisticated minority (in Vicino's case, invented by and for an audience of one) whose education predisposed them to think in allegories and conceits, and there is nothing intrinsically irrational about them, except the scale and the setting, which Vicino meant to be astonishing. His desire to go down in history as the maker of the eighth wonder of the world is recorded over and over again in verse on the rocks of Bomarzo. The voice of the duke—for there seems little doubt that the lines are his—whispers continually through the garden, promising and asking for stupefaction:

He who passes through this place
without raised eyebrows

and an open mouth
will be even less astonished
by the seven wonders of the world.

Reflect on this,
part by part,
you who enter here;
then tell me whether so many
marvels
were made by trickery,
or by art.

Vicino had no doubt that his garden was unique:

Memphis and all the other marvels
that the world esteems give way to the
Sacred Wood,
which resembles only itself and
nothing else.

The recluse of Bomarzo had indeed produced an incomparable work of art. There is nothing else like it. But before asking where he got the idea for his garden, we might consider what the idea of a *meraviglia* meant to a cultivated person in mid-sixteenth-century Italy, and what it did not mean.

Looking back on the past, we automatically tinge it with the dye of our own cultural assumptions. The elaborate artificiality of Mannerism, for example, has been taken as an index of strain by critics for the last fifty years, and the irrationalities of modern art—especially of surrealism—are wished back onto a style that did not in fact

share them. In Mannerist art, whether tiny, like a Cellini ring, or vast, like the Bomarzo gardens, the idea of a marvel centers on virtuosity. This was a conscious game. You selected, or better still invented, a formal problem whose difficulty would be obvious to a cultivated audience and then solved it with grace and ostentatious ease. The essential dialogue in Mannerist style was between the difficulty of the problem and the facility of the solution. The issues were fully understood. With surrealism, this exalted status of style did not exist: the surrealist was apt to find an image "marvelous" because its maker did not understand it; the image was esteemed as the trace of impulses that play through an artist in his role as medium for the Unconscious. Thus a marvel is not deliberately shaped, not controlled; it is the product of a chance encounter in an odd context.

By contrast, the sixteenth-century patron marveled at consciously deployed skill. Extravagance proved the artist's ingenuity, and part of this ingenuity was a field of literary cross-references. Since most modern art does not appeal to a literary culture, it is not necessary to assume that the viewer has sets of such references in his head. A split has opened between sensual and conceptual discourse. Mannerism presupposed their unity. Hence Bomarzo seems to have

Siren, Hypnerotomachia Poliphili

Her twin tails spread along the ground, a colossal siren watches over the Sacred Wood.

Many sixteenth-century artists and garden designers drew inspiration from the *Hypnerotomachia* woodcuts, and it seems likely that Orsini had them in mind when he directed the carving of his Bomarzo sculptures. Fortuna borne by a tortoise (opposite, far left) is similar to the figure of Fortuna atop an obelisk opposite; the siren at right, although she has no wings, bears a striking resemblance to the woodcut above.

straddled the literary and visual cultures of its time, in an often second-rate and derivative but always quirkish and unexpected way. Fictional gardens may well have given a cue to the creator of the Sacred Wood.

Vicino was an eclectic. That is clear from the sculpture he commissioned: the Michelangelesque giants, the oriental motifs, the zoo of images. And in his time it would not have been possible to be a dilettante for long without encountering one of the most admired books of the sixteenth century, the *Hypnerotomachia Poliphili*, or *Love, Dream, and Battle of Poliphilo*, which was published in 1499 and is believed to have been written by a Venetian monk named Francesco Colonna. The *Hypnerotomachia,* a long, obscure, and almost impenetrable allegory, enjoyed a wide circulation among humanists and scholars in Italy, France, and England. It tells of a man who, in search of his ideal lover, Polia, begins in a trackless and frightening wood, emerges from it parched with thirst, falls asleep, passes through two successive layers or states of dreaming, and awakens in an ideal garden-landscape, strewn with odd monuments and the ruins of antique temples. He has come to the fairy realm of Queen Eleuterilda, where, after a great deal of allegorical maneuvering, Polia at last appears to him in the form of a nymph, and

they are blissfully united. In a number of ways the *Hypnerotomachia,* being fundamentally an allegory of the descent, purification, and rebirth of consciousness, resembled other medieval and Renaissance literary monuments, notably Dante's *Divine Comedy,* with which it has in common, to name only four aspects, the vision of the ideal lady (Beatrice in Dante, Polia in the *Hypnerotomachia*), the initiation by terror in a dark wood, the sleeping fits that lead to new revelations, and the guide.

The *Hypnerotomachia* was liberally illustrated with woodcuts, showing the ruins, statues, masques, inscriptions, and processions that Poliphilo encountered. They are very detailed and explicit. Plate after plate is devoted to close-ups of the ornaments on Cupid's chariot, or the temple in which Poliphilo is scared by a dragon; and some two hundred inscriptions, of stupefying length and prolixity, are "recorded" from graves in the Polyandrion, a classical cemetery that he and Polia visit. The plates in the *Hypnerotomachia* had an immense influence over the way people thought about gardens in the sixteenth and seventeenth centuries, and they can also be shown to have inspired famous monuments of the time—Bernini's elephant carrying an obelisk in Rome, for instance, derives from a cut in the *Hypnerotomachia.*

In Colonna's work lies one origin of the artificial ruin as garden architecture, which became such a cult with landscape architects of the eighteenth century. And it seems possible that Vicino Orsini remembered this book while designing his valley at Bomarzo. For in valley as in text we have a collection of allegorical marvels, copiously inscribed with references to dreams, the spirits of a sacred wood, and initiation by amazement. And there are many similarities of detail between the *Hypnerotomachia*'s woodcuts and Vicino's designs in Bomarzo. The dragon Poliphilo meets in the temple may be reflected in Bomarzo's dragon; the siren in the valley, twirling her tails, is—allowing for a slight difference of graphic flourishes not transferable to three dimensions—the exact sister of a detail in the *Hypnerotomachia*; and the effigy of Fortuna that Poliphilo sees balanced on an obelisk above a temple in Queen Eleuterilda's demesne may have suggested Vicino's Lady Luck on tortoise-back, rising majestically above the trees. Even the profusion of texts and mottoes carved on Bomarzo's rocks reminds one of the inscriptions with which Poliphilo's dreamland is so generously dotted. They serve to mark points in the narrative just as Vicino's inscriptions stop you in the garden, and one reason he takes four hundred pages

A stone titan, some twenty feet high (above and at right), grapples with another giant in Orsini's Sacred Wood. Carved from an enormous rock and covered with lichen, the sculpture seems to grow right out of the earth.

to finish his dream is that he is always halting to read the writing on the wall.

Yet it would narrow the garden and do injustice to the breadth of Vicino's fantasies to try to locate all its images within one book. The Enchanted Forest, the Sacred Wood, was one of the favorite themes of Italian literature. It occurs, to name only two sixteenth-century writers whom Vicino may have read, in Bernardo Tasso's *Amadigi* and Torquato Tasso's *Gerusalemme liberata*. By the same token, some Bomarzo sculptures that have no parallel in the *Hypnerotomachia* could have derived from any one of a dozen written sources. Is the whale the Biblical cetacean, for instance? Or is it the sea beast on which Ariosto's hero Astolfo sets foot, in mistake for secure land? Some images may be historical: the attacked dragon with its crescent wingornaments may refer to the defeat of the Turks at Lepanto, which happened while work on Bomarzo was in progress, and it is difficult to explain the elephant, crushing its victim clad in ancient Roman armor, except as an allusion to Hannibal's campaign. The huge mask, whose inscribed mouth promises the restful cessation of all thought (or perhaps the ironic impossibility of communicating with posterity: *Ogni pensiero vola* indeed), is a familiar Mannerist architectural motif, and the same

image exists in openings to doors and windows of the Palazzo Zuccari in Rome. It is the once terrible symbol of hell's gate, deprived of its power by Mannerist wit and transformed into a garden kiosk with a table for picnicking.

Of the artists who carved these fables, nothing is known. The legend that the work was done by Turkish prisoners of war from Lepanto may be dismissed out of hand, since figurative sculpture did not flourish among those people, whose religion forbade the making of images. There are no signatures, several hands seem to have been involved, and various minor artists in the circle of Michelangelo, each less convincing than the last, have been proposed. But there is one interesting possibility about the sculptures. Some, if not all, of the shapes may have been "released" from what the artist (or more likely his master, Vicino) saw lurking in the natural form of the boulders, strewn *in situ* down the valley. A famous passage in Leonardo da Vinci's notebooks adumbrates this:

If you look at any walls spotted with various stains or with a mixture of different kinds of stones, if you are about to invent some scene . . . you will also be able to see divers combats and figures in quick movement, and strange expressions of faces, and outlandish costumes, and an infinite number of things which you can then reduce to separate and well-conceived forms. With such walls and blends of different stones it comes about as it does with the sound of bells, in whose clanging you may discover every name and word that you can imagine.

Bomarzo is an ambiguous place, and the cliffs above its valley can still reveal, under some lights, the contours of mask and grimace, coifed with wild tufts of trees against the skyline. The prodigies of Vicino's Sacred Wood may have risen to greet him from the stones themselves. But we will never know for certain; and perhaps it is not such a pity, for the pleasures of Bomarzo still depend, for pedant and surrealist alike, on the elusiveness of its meaning.

In our Winter issue Robert Hughes defended the grandeur of Beaux-Arts architecture.

The Decline of Common Sense

And why we might wish to revive it

DRAWING BY HONORE DAUMIER: MUSEE DES BEAUX-ARTS — REIMS-GIRAUDON

Common sense is usually said to be sturdy, but in fact it has been faring badly ever since the Scientific Revolution began. It is plain, common sense declared in those days, that the sun revolves around the earth. Wrong, said Copernicus, and of course the astronomer was right. It is plain, said common sense, undaunted, that heavy bodies fall faster than light ones. Wrong, said Galileo, and of course Galileo was right.

So it has been for the past four hundred years. Every time a new science took command of a subject, common sense had to retreat. When the dismal science of economics was founded, common sense, it turned out, did not even understand money. By the time Ibsen was ready to proclaim that "a majority is always wrong," the authority of common sense had clearly reached some sort of nadir. There it remains to this day, and no one seems to care as much as I think we should. We live, said George Orwell, in a "yogi-ridden age," an age when every kind of mountebank, quack, and nostrum peddler can gather himself a sizable congregation—occasionally even an entire nation. Surely this is true, in part, because common sense has lost its grip.

Just what is common sense anyway that its decline should merit concern? This turns out to be a difficult question; common sense is far easier to recognize than define. An abstract definition, for one thing, is hardly in keeping with its spirit, for common sense itself is

Don Quixote and Sancho: "pointing the way to unfathomable depths"

unreflective, the "unthinking reasonableness" of humanity, according to Hegel, perhaps its last philosophical admirer. A purely personal conception of common sense would do even greater violence to its spirit, for personal and private judgments, the fruits of mere self, are the common enemies of common sense. They are exactly what common sense irons out like so many wrinkles in a shirt.

The ironing-out process seems to work somewhat as follows. Ask twelve randomly chosen people to sit down together and reach a common judgment on some common human occurrence. Ask them, for example, whether a person who walked smack into a roadside pothole did or did not bear some blame for his fractured shinbone. At first, and almost inevitably, the extremists will dominate the discussion. One of the group, scathing in his contempt for fools, insists that anyone stupid enough to walk into a pothole should count

himself lucky he still has a neck. A second person, equally scathing in his contempt for government, asserts that any public official who failed to fill a pothole merits public censure and instant recall. Others in the group, holding middling views, will emphasize the contingent, qualifying facts in the case at hand.

In the exchange of views, the contemner of fools sees that he has grown a bit hard-hearted. The denouncer of officialdom learns that road maintenance is more difficult than he had supposed. Indeed, in the course of the discussion, everyone will surrender some of his cherished private notions. A common judgment is reached, and it is the judgment of common sense. It is based on what the twelve conferees hold in common, after discarding what is not, about humankind's moral and civic responsibilities as they pertain to walking on and repairing roadways.

I am, of course, describing the deliberations of a jury in a negligence suit. Yet what is the jury system if not a monument to our faith in common sense (and what is the modern impatience with juries if not testimony to our loss of that faith). The jury room is a forcing-house for reaching common-sense conclusions, and it plainly reveals the essential point about common sense. It is *not* the sense of commoners. It is the sense that is found to be common when the facts of the case are inspected from any number of personal viewpoints. The

By WALTER KARP

origin of common sense is simply humankind's faculty for talking and exchanging views. It is the deliberations of a vast, diverse jury charged with rendering a sober verdict on human life, human nature, and human passions.

Prideful people, understandably, dislike serving on juries, for common sense is a fierce humbler of pride and egotism. It tells the man with a theory that he has left out a salient fact. It reminds the man with the eccentric viewpoint to shift his watching post a little and take a second look. The great virtue of common sense is amplitude. Common sense does not take in everything, but it never omits much of importance. When it thinks of wealth it remembers poverty, and when it thinks of play it will not forget toil.

Common sense remembers, too, that human pleasures are not so plentiful when anyone tries to snatch one away. Take, for example, the common-sense view of vegetarianism. The vegetarian dwells on slaughterhouse horrors and willingly forgoes the pleasures of food, society, and shared festivities. Common sense holds fast to those pleasures and will not, in this vale of tears, put a cattle market at the center of life. It even suspects that an uncommon empathy for fatted calves masks a want of common affection for people. Common sense holds, in other words, that all discussions of diet are shallow unless we consider the effects of diet on fellow feeling, which is to say, on something more important than food.

To say that common sense has lost its grip is to say that prideful people and one-sided views hold undue sway in our councils. The prideful take up, for example, the "problem of the unfit parent." As usual with the prideful, they grasp the wrong end of the telescope, for the real question, the profound question, the common-sense question, is why so many parents are fit. Why is it that, despite all the temptations of flesh and spirit, despite the ineradicable fact of human selfishness, more parents cherish, protect, and nurture their children and devote the best years of their lives to them? It is the common-sense question because it starts with the rule and not with the exception. This is the real meaning of the adage about the exception "proving" the rule. Starting with the rule is the first rule of common sense and defines its indispensable function: to remember the comprehensive facts in the case, the facts that most faithfully summarize our shared experience of life, what Dr. Johnson called our "general nature."

Someone once mentioned to Johnson a certain person who claimed to see no distinction between virtue and vice. To which Johnson replied: "If he does really think that there is no distinction between virtue and vice, why, Sir, when he leaves our houses let us count our spoons." This is, I think, a perfect example of common sense set to work, albeit by an uncommon man who wielded it like a club. A prideful conceit makes its appearance and common sense subjects it to the comprehensive fact: if we didn't distinguish between virtue and vice, no one could trust another and the whole system of life would fall apart.

Common sense, then, is adamantly antihistorical. It insists implicitly that nothing fundamental really changes much. Birds of a feather will still flock together, pride will still go before a fall, an ounce of prevention will still be worth a pound of cure, and our general nature will still be visible under any cloak that history fashions for it. What, after all, do Homer's heroes have in common with us? Nothing, except pride, vanity, courage, friendship, fear, anger, folly, and mortality.

It is here, however, that common sense and modern thinking have most widely drifted apart. The modern mind is history-minded. It dwells not on permanence but on change. It sees humankind submerged in history, created by history, altered perpetually by history. From the viewpoint of modern thinking, the comprehensive facts of our general nature hardly seem very important. They appear to be a sort of lumpish residue left behind by the historical process and consisting chiefly of trifling truisms about birds of a feather and the like.

This view is a perilously shallow one. The facts that common sense grasps are often the truly deep and marvelous ones. The rule always cuts deeper than the exception. Any clever sociologist can (and will) get up an explanation of crime, but it would take more than a clever sociologist to explain the real mystery, which is why most people are law-abiding. Similarly, any ingenious psychologist can produce an explanation of suicide, but who will explain nonsuicide? Even the intrepid Aristotle gave up any thought of trying. "There must be something sweet about life," he concluded, "or men would not cling to it so." Is there a general proposition more profound, more rich in wonder, than this common-sense observation?

A truly surprising paradox is implied in all this. Prideful thought and common sense stand at opposite poles, yet the poles turn out to be the very reverse of what they seem at first glance. It is vaunting prideful thought, the thought of singular people, that usually ends in a cut-and-dried syllogism, and it is plodding, worldly common sense that leads to mysteries beyond rational solution.

No one has rendered this paradox more beautifully than Cervantes. His Don Quixote represents all that is noble and silly in vaunting singular pride and in a life bravely lived according to one's own stock of notions. Quixote himself adheres to a quite systematic, if comical, ideology—the rules and principles of chivalric romance. At the end of his long adventure in the chivalric system, however, Quixote takes to his bed with a common-sense proverb on his lips. "There are no birds this year in last year's nests," he wearily reminds his faithful companion. It is Sancho Panza, who represents all that is earthbound and commonsensical, who begs Quixote with tears in his eyes to get out of bed and go roving once more. So reason, the product of one man's communion with himself, ends with a bump on the solid earth, while common sense, the product of humankind gossiping around the village pump, points the way to unfathomable depths.

Gypsies

With a portfolio of portraits by Josef Koudelka

Gypsy caravan, Czechoslovakia, 1965

Wordsworth called the Gypsies "wild outcasts of society." In the folklore of the nineteenth and twentieth centuries, they appear mainly in the guise of dark-haired, mysterious fortunetellers and colorfully dressed violinists, ready to break into song at the drop of a coin.

The Gypsies are more—a misunderstood, unknown, coherent yet dissimilar group of people spread throughout the world. Their origins are obscure, their numbers today are uncounted, and uncountable. For nearly a millennium they have existed on the outskirts of society, living apart through choice, but exiled also by the prejudices of others.

The precise origin of the Gypsies has never been discovered. Ethnological and linguistic studies ascribe their homeland to the Indus Basin in northern India, where, sometime around A.D. 1000, a westward migration began, prompted perhaps by a local political disturbance. Fragmentary evidence has placed the Gypsies in Crete around 1322, in Corfu before 1326, and in other areas of the Balkans before the end of the fourteenth century. Such evidence is barely credible. The Friar Simon who supposedly encountered the Gypsies in

Crete in 1322 wrote merely that he had seen "a people outside the city who declare themselves to be of the race of Ham . . . They wander like a cursed people from place to place, not stopping at all or rarely in one place longer than thirty days."

More solid documentation exists for the arrival of a band of some two hundred Gypsies near Hamburg, Germany, in 1417, and another group of a hundred or so on the outskirts of Paris in 1427. There, a contemporaneous chronicler recorded that they were "the poorest creatures ever seen coming to France within the memory of man . . . And in the end they had to go away . . ." The dispersal of the Gypsies had begun.

Bands of Gypsies spread across the continent and eventually to the New World, carrying with them their customs and their ancient language, Romany, thought for centuries to be nothing more than a thieves' jargon. (It is in fact, an Indo-European language, though unrelated to Rumanian or to the family of Romance languages.) As a migrant people, they became convenient scapegoats for local problems and untold ills. Henry VIII of England, taking

time out from his problems with the Church of Rome, decreed a ban against further immigration of the "outland-ysshe People," and his daughter Elizabeth ordered Gypsies living in England to leave within forty days, because of "their old accustomed devilish and naughty Practices."

The "devilish and naughty" practice that most worried Their Royal Highnesses of England and elsewhere was fortunetelling. When the Gypsies appeared in Paris in 1427, they had "looked into people's hands and told what had happened to them, or would happen." The bishop of Paris, alarmed at such disobedience on the part of his flock, forthwith declared that any Parisian who went to a Gypsy to hear the future would be excommunicated. Despite such disapprobation, Gypsy fortunetelling continues to this day. A sign on the sidewalk of my block in New York City proclaims, "Reader and Advisor." Occasionally I see children, dark-haired and poorly dressed, outside that building. Are they Gypsies? I do not know. But when I see them, I recall a suggestion made by Jan Yoors, who ran away from home in the 1930's, at the age

TEXT CONTINUED ON PAGE 69

By KAETHE ELLIS

Spain, 1972

Rumania, 1968

of twelve, to join a band of Gypsies. He writes that fortunetelling is a means of survival for a people who have little or no other recourse:

The Rom [the Gypsies' word for themselves] certainly gained a degree of self-protection from the Gaje's [or *gadje*'s, i.e., non-Gypsy's] fear of the Gypsies' curses and spells. In a subtle way it could limit the brutality and the repression inflicted on a minority without adequate defense. The legal status of the Gypsies was at best that of a tolerated minority, at worst that of undesirables to be extradited or eliminated, and at the mercy of all. By fortune-telling they imposed on the credulous a certain fear and respect: a slim defense but better than nothing.

Recourse is necessary, for the Gypsies have endured vilification comparable to that encountered by the blacks and the Jews. During World War II, Adolf Hitler, ignoring all possible definitions of the word "Aryan," grouped Gypsies with "Jews, racial inferiors, and asocials," banishing them first to concentration camps and eventually ordering their wholesale extermination. Estimates of the number of Gypsies executed by Hitler run as high as 500,000. It is impossible to verify this figure. However, out of forty-five hundred Gypsies at Auschwitz, some two thousand were gassed on the night of August 2, 1944, and another 915 were transferred to Buchenwald for lethal experiments in drinking sea water.

Today, despite persecution and experimentation, despite banishment and extermination, the Gypsies survive, and may be propagating their own faster than ever before. In 1968 a Czechoslovakian census showed that the Gypsy population was increasing at the rate of more than 2.6 per cent, in contrast to the national birth rate of 0.4 per cent. Current estimates of the number of Gypsies in the United States range from 250,000 to more than a million, constituting an underground populace that lives by its own rules and believes first and foremost in its own societal mores.

CARTIER-BRESSON—MAGNUM

Josef Koudelka

Josef Koudelka has been following and photographing Gypsies for fifteen years—in Czechoslovakia, where he was born in 1938, and in Rumania, Spain, and other western European countries. Each year when the weather turns warm enough for him to sleep outdoors near Gypsy settlements, he seeks out their camps, where he says he is received with a mixture of tolerance, suspicion, and—since who would live this way if he didn't have to?—pity. His friend Cartier-Bresson took the photograph at left.

Those mores are, in many ways, stricter than the rules we—the *gadje*—live by. They are based on a patriarchal society (the word "Rom" is also the word for "man"), on an endogamous, or inbred, society, on a society that lives in constant proximity. A family group among Gypsies is all-important, and cannot be separated. Yoors recounts an incident in which the local gendarmes raided the camp he lived in:

Under the sneering supervision of the officers, the Gypsies were compelled to travel in the directions of the four winds, with total disregard for their family allegiances. . . . It struck me that the Rom departed without taking leave of one another. In time I found out that after a few days they would change their courses, stray for a while, and then one day they all would converge and meet again, in numbers too large for the local police to cope with. They were like the quicksilver that constantly merges and divides.

Gypsy society is self-governed by the *kris*, a Romany word that denotes a body of law and custom—comprising usage, oral traditions, and magical practices—and also a local tribunal that judges tribal infractions. Major violations of the unwritten code of rules by which the Gypsies live, such as consorting with the *gadje*, are punished by *marima*, in which a man and his family are ostracized from the tribe. Other taboos, akin to those of the Old Testament, extend to personal cleanliness and sexual practices—reflecting the necessity for strict controls within their closed, nomadic society.

And what of Gypsies today? Have we —the *gadje*—progressed beyond the age-old notion of Gypsies as vagabonds,

thieves, whirling dancers, musicians, and con men? Are we to accept Peter Maas's account of Steve Tene, the self-styled heir of the king of the Bimbo clan of Gypsies in New Jersey? Despite Maas's sympathy for the problems of Gypsies, he has produced a book that upholds the equation of Gypsies and thieves.

Are we to listen to a Czech dictionary published in 1951 that defines a Gypsy as "a member of a nomadic nation, symbol of mendacity, thievery, a vagabond; metaphorically— a liar, imposter"? Czechoslovakia is currently embarked on a solution to the "Gypsy problem." The government's proposal requires assimilation of Gypsies into the national ethnic group. In a recent survey, however, a woman of twenty-five, identified as a working-class woman with a basic education, is quoted as saying, "In a few years our town will be a Gypsy town, the white people will have to move out because it is not possible to live among the Gypsies." The rhetoric is, to say the least, familiar.

There is, I think, no definitive answer. Gypsies inhabit the world today, just as they inhabited the world of the fifteenth century. They were not accepted then, nor are they accepted today. They have changed their life style to a certain degree: horses and wagons have been traded in for RV's—recreational vehicles—that serve as mobile homes. But they remain a separate community.

An old Gypsy proverb declares that "God knows what tomorrow will bring." That, more than anything, characterizes the Gypsies. Perhaps we should not worry about the future of the Gypsies; rather, we should accept the philosophy they themselves have adopted. As Jan Yoors wrote in 1967, "The Rom lived in a perpetual present: memories, dreams, desires, hungers, the urge toward a tomorrow, all were rooted in the present. Without *now* there was no before, just as there could be no *after*." In the end, the quicksilver will remain.

THE GLORY THAT WAS THRACE

Treasures from this ancient, savage land come westward in an extraordinary new exhibition

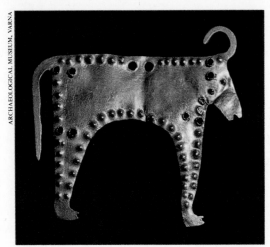

Gold was worked in Thrace as early as 3200 B.C. Above, a small animal plaque, possibly the oldest gold object ever found in Europe. Opposite, a gold-and-silver face from a piece of armor (see page 74).

Among the allies of the Trojans in the bitter war to save their city were men from the far-off land of Thrace. Their king possessed, as one character in the *Iliad* reported:

the biggest and handsomest horses
  I ever saw,
whiter than snow and swifter than
  the winds,
and a chariot finely wrought with
  silver and gold.
The arms he came with are also of gold. . . .

A taste for war, for silver and gold, for fine horses—Homer caught features that were to mark the Thracians throughout their history.

The area the Thracians occupied coincides roughly with Bulgaria, the European part of Turkey, and the northeastern portion of Greece. It embraces coastal plains along the north Aegean and the left-hand corner of the Black Sea, upland plains inland, and ranges of steep mountains, notably the Balkans. Flints and other artifacts attest that people were living here back in the Stone Age, forty thousand years ago. The next discoverable inhabitants appear much later, a Neolithic race with precocious skills. Archaeologists have dug up ample evidence not only of farming and herding but of the sculptor's and metalworker's craft; among the finds are well-fashioned bracelets, necklaces, and other adornments of gold that date from a time shortly before 3000 B.C.

What happened to these gifted Neo-

By LIONEL CASSON

PHOTOGRAPHS BY ERICH LESSING

A

Tumulus, or burial mound, near Kazanlŭk

A Thracian mercenary

Much of the wealth on these pages comes from burial sites like the one above. The pottery idol at right survives from a pre-Thracian culture that vanished with the arrival of the Bronze Age. The fifth-century Athenian kylix, top right, bears the figure of a Thracian peltast (named for his crescent-shaped shield, or pelta), employed by the Greeks as a mercenary. The inscription on the ring, lower right, is in Greek letters, since the Thracians never developed their own alphabet.

A pottery idol, circa 3000 B.C.

A Thracian inscription

lithic folk is not known. The Thracians that Homer had heard of, those sumptuously armed, hard-driving warriors, appear on the scene a few centuries before the Trojan War, about 1500 or perhaps a bit sooner. They were intruders who, since they spoke an Indo-European tongue (i.e., one akin to Latin and Greek and other well known European languages), must have come from the Indo-European homeland to the east, but from precisely where—and why—is anybody's guess. Homer's talk of their wealth is no mere poetic fancy: they too were well aware of the country's mineral resources. Near the town of Vulchitrun in northern Bulgaria a farmer turning the soil for a vineyard in 1924 blundered upon what must have been the grave of a Thracian chieftain of the period—and the objects he unearthed are astounding: a collection of more than a dozen bowls, cups, covers, and disks of solid gold weighing more than twenty-seven pounds in all; one bowl alone weighs close to nine. The leaders of this obscure people went to their eternal rest in hardly less luxury than their celebrated contemporaries to the south who were buried in the "Tomb of Agamemnon," the "Tomb of Clytemnestra," and the other magnificent chambers that Heinrich Schliemann found in Mycenaean Greece.

Inevitably, these opulent chieftains and their tribesmen were sucked into the churning of peoples that took place between 1200 and 1000 B.C. when unidentified invaders, sweeping over the eastern Mediterranean, shattered the Mycenaean Greeks and the Hittites, sapped the strength of Egypt, and brought the curtain down on the Bronze Age. When the first act of the Iron Age opens, the cast of characters is significantly different. The Mycenaean Greeks have been replaced by their later relatives who will play so crucial a role in the formation of Western culture. And the Thracians of the *Iliad* re-emerge as one of the many races who, inhabiting lands beyond the ken of the Greeks and speaking a language incomprehensible to them, were called by them "barbarians." These particular barbarians, moreover, were primitives in Greek eyes since they spurned urban life and, maintaining their age-old tribal organization, lived in villages that were mere aggregations of huts and supported themselves by farming, herding, hunting, and brigandage. As it happens, it was their contact with the Greeks that finally brought them out of the shadows of epic poetry and archaeology and into the light of history.

Between roughly 700 and 600 B.C. the Greek city-states were sending out colonists so assiduously that they ended up planting settlements all around the eastern Mediterranean and the Black Sea. When they landed on the shores of the north Aegean and the Black Sea just beyond the Bosporus, they ran into Thracians, and it took savage fighting and spilling of much blood on both sides before these Thracians yielded their rights of possession and grudgingly retreated into the mountains that flanked the coastal plains. Much later, the Athenians, at a moment when theirs was the most powerful of the Greek city-states, needed two tries to found a colony at a strategic point where trade routes crossed not far from some gold mines; the first time, the ten thousand they sent were wiped out to a man. The better-armed and better-organized Greeks eventually established footholds, and Abdera and Aenus on the Aegean, Apollonia and Odessus on the Black Sea, and other ports swiftly became flourishing cities that carried on an active trade with the natives in the hinterland.

Around the middle of the fifth century B.C. that insatiably curious Greek traveler Herodotus visited Thrace, and from his pen we get the earliest firsthand report on its people. What impressed him most were their religious idiosyncrasies. Like all Greeks, Herodotus worshiped many gods, the more the better, and had a healthy preference for this world over any hypothetically joyous hereafter; hence he was astonished to learn that certain Thracian tribes were not merely monotheists but, no question

Mold for casting a bronze scepter

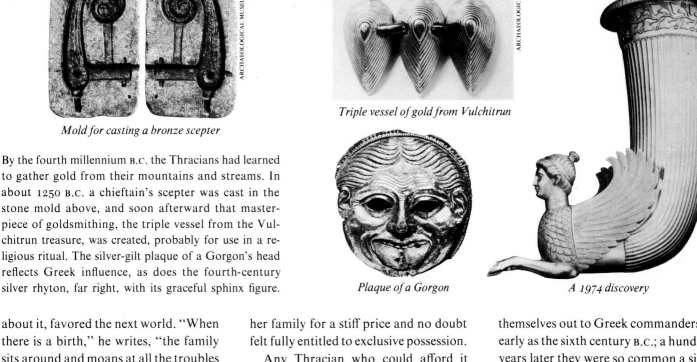

Triple vessel of gold from Vulchitrun

Plaque of a Gorgon

A 1974 discovery

By the fourth millennium B.C. the Thracians had learned to gather gold from their mountains and streams. In about 1250 B.C. a chieftain's scepter was cast in the stone mold above, and soon afterward that masterpiece of goldsmithing, the triple vessel from the Vulchitrun treasure, was created, probably for use in a religious ritual. The silver-gilt plaque of a Gorgon's head reflects Greek influence, as does the fourth-century silver rhyton, far right, with its graceful sphinx figure.

about it, favored the next world. "When there is a birth," he writes, "the family sits around and moans at all the troubles the infant, now that it has been born, must go through . . . ; when there is a death, they bury the body with joking and merrymaking, pointing out the evils he has left in exchange for total bliss." Another way the Thracians differed from the Greeks was in practicing polygamy. When a man died, his favorite wife would be slaughtered and put in the grave along with him. Since this ensured an accelerated entry into eternal happiness, there was such competition for the honor that friends of the family had to help decide which of the widows had been the most beloved. (Sometimes more than one qualified: a grave at Vratsa has yielded the bodies of a young couple, the woman with a knife in her chest. In an outer chamber was found another woman with a spear through hers.) Herodotus also notes that the Thracians followed the practice, scorned by Greeks, of tattooing themselves, the higher the rank, the more the markings. Thracian sexual behavior, too, was very un-Greek: Greek men insisted on virgin brides, whereas Thracian girls were allowed all the sexual partners they wanted. Marriage, to be sure, changed this. Then the boom came down with a vengeance since, among other considerations, a prospective groom had to purchase his bride from

her family for a stiff price and no doubt felt fully entitled to exclusive possession.

Any Thracian who could afford it held farming in vast contempt and considered fighting, principally brigandage, to be the sole proper source of income. Then the Greeks arrived, and there was plenty of gainful employment available as soon as it became apparent that the Thracians' native arms and tactics neatly complemented the Greeks'. Greek armies specialized in heavily armed infantrymen—the famous hoplites. They were chronically short of cavalry and had no lightly armed troops at all. The Thracians had a plethora of horsemen, and those among them who fought on foot wore no breastplate but just a thigh-length tunic, no helmet but just the traditional Thracian peaked cap of fox fur, and no greaves but just the traditional Thracian soft leather boots. Their only defensive armor was a very light crescent-shaped shield, usually made of nothing heavier than wicker covered with hide; it was called a pelta, and the men equipped with it were dubbed peltasts. They carried a short curved saber and either a pair of javelins or a long thrusting spear. Completely mobile, they made ideal guerrillas—and the Greeks discovered that the best way of protecting their solid slow-moving lines of hoplites from them was to fight fire with fire and have some peltasts on their own side. Thracians began hiring

themselves out to Greek commanders as early as the sixth century B.C.; a hundred years later they were so common a sight on the streets of Athens that Aristophanes could make jokes about them: one of Lysistrata's comrades in the sex strike tells how she saw a Thracian buck come swaggering into the marketplace

and, brandishing spear and pelta, make
    some fruitseller so afraid
she takes to her heels—and lets him take
    her total stock in trade.

The Thracians profoundly affected the Greek art of war. By the fourth century B.C., all city-states were using sizable contingents of peltasts, made up of Greeks as well as Thracians.

There was yet another way Thracians came to be a common sight in Greece— as slaves. Male prisoners of war were often put on the block, and both males and females became available through the Thracians' practice, remarked on by Herodotus, of exporting their children for the market. As a consequence, numbers of Thracians were to be found in the service of Greek families. They must have stood out among their short, dark owners, for they were relatively tall, gray-eyed, and either fair-haired or red-haired. Maids and valets in Greek plays often bear such names as Thratta and Geta; *Thratta* is simply the Greek for "Thracian girl," and the Getae were among the most important Thracian tribes. The slaves as well as the soldiers were grist for the comic playwright's mill. In one scene Menander has a slave named Geta hold forth on the Thracians' superiority to all those unfortunate men who have to do with but one wife: "We have ten, eleven, twelve, even more. Why, back home any poor devil who has only four or five doesn't even count as married."

By the fifth century B.C. we find ambitious chieftains of major tribes promoting themselves into kings by overpowering their neighbors. In the 420's, for example, a certain Sitalces managed to take over most of the country, not excepting the Greek cities along the coast. Since the Athenians had important interests in the area he controlled, though they were at the height of their strength and influence, they wooed him as passionately as we do Third World nations today, sending full-fledged embassies to his court, even declaring his son an honorary citizen. His successor managed to build up the crown's annual take in gold and silver—consisting of the tribute levied upon the subjugated tribes and Greek cities, together with the "presents" they were constantly being called upon to give—to a grand total of eight hundred talents, two hundred more than Athens collected from all the

subjects in her empire during Pericles' greatest days. Probably not much of it filtered down to the rank and file, but the nobility certainly got their share, to judge by the many tumuli, mounds marking the graves of chieftains or powerful members of their following. Dating from the sixth century B.C. right down to the days of the Roman Empire, these tombs are carefully built of squared stone and are often lavishly decorated inside with wall paintings. Furthermore, just as in earlier times, the deceased was laid to rest amid a wealth of precious objects. There is one significant difference, however: by this time Thrace had been in contact with Greek civilization, and, as a result, many of the objects were things the dead man had purchased from Greek craftsmen or had had Greeks make for him. Those from the hands of local workmen very often mingle Greek and native elements. The country was becoming Hellenized.

We can tell how pervasive the process was from Xenophon's account of his experiences in Thrace. He arrived there in 400 B.C. with the remainder of the ten thousand Greek soldiers he had led in the celebrated march through Asia Minor's rugged terrain and hostile tribes to the safety of the Black Sea. An ambitious chieftain named Seuthes

hired almost all of them, figuring—rightly, as it turned out—that, with his local cavalry and lightly armed troops stiffened by the toughest contingent of hoplites in existence, he would have no trouble gaining control of the country. Even though, as Xenophon pointedly observes, Seuthes was well able to follow most of what was said in Greek, the negotiations were conducted through an interpreter. At a banquet that Seuthes gave, the server of the wine spoke Greek. The Hellenization did not penetrate very far, however, as the banquet itself shows; it was decidedly in the native style. The main dish was meat served with huge loaves of bread, and the host helped his guests along by tossing chunks of both at them. Wine was drunk from horns and the custom was, after draining a hornful, to splash the last drops over oneself. Music was supplied by army trumpets and by what Xenophon describes as "trumpets of raw oxhide" (were they bagpipes?), and the moment it started Seuthes leaped up and did a war dance. The Thracians also had a sword dance, a pas de deux with sabers in which the performers mimed a duel with such verisimilitude that, when one fell, audiences often thought he was really dead. Death actually did sometimes take place

TEXT CONTINUED ON PAGE 79

ARMS, OPULENCE, AND A DOUBLE MURDER

The People's Republic of Bulgaria, once the heartland of ancient Thrace, is currently sending an exhibition of about a thousand archaeological treasures to various capital cities in the Western world. Almost all the objects have been discovered since 1879, when Bulgaria became independent of the Ottoman Empire, and some were excavated as recently as last year. Dating from the fourth millennium B.C. to the days of the Roman occupation of Thrace in the third century A.D., they echo the art of central Europe as well as that of nearby Greece, Persia, and the lands of the Scythians. On the opening pages of this article appears a female Thracian face (A) from the exhibition, executed in gold and silver to form part of a shin guard. It was found in the fourth-century B.C. tomb of a thirty-year-old man at Vratsa. (Two women, violently slain, were buried with him.) Opposite is a bronze helmet and cuirass (B) from about the sixth century B.C. The centaur on the following page (C) rests its hooves on the rim of a gold amphora-rhyton made in about 300 B.C., probably in Hellenistic Asia Minor. The six silver-gilt plaques (D) served as horse-harness decorations in the fourth century B.C., and the life-size helmet-mask of silver, bronze, and iron (E) was worn on parade during the Roman period. The exhibition has already been to London, Paris, Vienna, Moscow, and Leningrad.

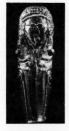

A

B

C

D

E

C

D

in one of the games the Thracians went in for, their version, as it were, of Russian roulette. A man would stand on a stone with one of the traditional Thracian curved knives in his hand and put his head in a hangman's noose. Someone would kick the stone away, and the trick was to slash the cord before it was too late. Anyone not fast enough drew a big laugh from the crowd for his unfortunate lack of skill.

These wild and primitive ways of the Thracians helped to even the cultural score by profoundly affecting the Greeks in their religion. The gods this people believed in were as wild as themselves, they worshiped them with violent, emotion-packed rituals, and all this touched a responsive chord in Greek breasts. It was from Thrace—or so the Greeks believed—that Orpheus had come to Greece, that mysterious figure whose music had the uncanny power to render savage beasts tame, and Dionysus as well, the wine god whose followers celebrated his festivals with ceremonies that climaxed in a frenzied ecstasy. A Thracian goddess, Bendis, was equated with Artemis, and her rites were carried on in the heart of Piraeus, where Plato himself saw them.

From the second century B.C. on, Rome became the dominant city in the eastern Mediterranean region, and by the beginning of the Christian Era had annexed large parts of it. So far as Thrace was concerned, the Romans were at first content to do as the Greeks had done, confining their occupation to the coastal strips and leaving the hinterland to the local chieftains and kings. All they required were levies of Thracian cavalry and foot soldiers to serve in the armies and the opportunity to acquire Thracian slaves. These were, as might be imagined, particularly useful for training as gladiators. The one gladiator most of us know by name, Spartacus, was a Thracian.

Then, shortly before the middle of the first century A.D., the Roman emper-

ors, moved by widespread unrest among the tribes, took steps to seize the interior as well—and thereby triggered the urbanization of the country as one base after another was set up for the legions and one center after another for the administration. The pace quickened when, in A.D. 105–6, the emperor Trajan crossed the Danube and annexed what is today Rumania. Throughout Thrace Trajan not only elevated what had been

The Thracian Horseman, above in a statuette, was worshiped in Roman times. Later, in the Christian Era, the image was easily transformed into Saint George, a favorite saint of the Bulgarians.

mere villages into towns and cities but started any number of new settlements from scratch. The extensive Roman ruins still visible show how comprehensive the process was. At Oescus on the Danube along the northern boundary of Bulgaria, where a legion was stationed, there are the remains of a fort, two aqueducts, and a bath complex; at Nicopolis, not far from Veliko Tŭrnovo in north central Bulgaria just north of the Balkans, are the remains of a theatre, colonnade, forum, council house, and paved

streets; Serdica, Sofia today, was raised from a mere village and garnished with a governor's palace, a fort, baths, and temples.

The Romans carried out their program with characteristic organization and thoroughness. Yet something of old Thrace tenaciously lingered on, especially in the remoter sections. Language is a case in point. In the plains and along the valleys where urbanization progressed relentlessly, Greek steadily displaced the native Thracian. But up in the mountains it was spoken all during the Roman occupation, right into the sixth century A.D., when the Slavs arrived in the last of the great migrations from the steppes.

Religion reveals still other survivals from old Thrace. In the new towns, there sprang up temples and chapels for the worship of the Roman emperors, of Serapis, Mithras, and the multifarious other deities that Rome's subjects prayed to. But in the back country the ancient ways and gods held their own. Old-fashioned landowners still had themselves buried in the time-honored Thracian fashion, under a tumulus. The peasants still made obeisance to the gods of their ancestors, above all the "Thracian Horseman," so called because he is invariably represented as a horseman charging with a spear at some wild animal. When Christianity came, they simply transferred their allegiance to Saint George.

Indeed, the past is still very much alive in the hearts of the present inhabitants of the land. To remind the world of their heritage they have fashioned an exhibit of objects that display its long life and vicissitudes, from finely wrought massive gold pieces that predate the Egyptian pyramids to roughhewn stone reliefs of the Thracian Horseman made during the last days of the Roman Empire.

Lionel Casson, our man in ancient Greece and Rome, is professor of classics at NYU.

And Now, the Edifying Edifice

Fine art comes to the side of a barn

A pre-Tyler barn

People had been painting on barns long before the admen at Mail Pouch started using barn sides as billboards. But it was not until 1971 that anyone thought of decorating barns not for commerce but for art. The man who did it is an engaging twenty-six-year-old artist named Douglas Tyler. In 1969 Tyler, then an undergraduate at Michigan State, did his first wall painting—in a friend's bathroom—and soon afterward got a long ladder, lots of paint, and permission to put an outsized Mona Lisa on a barn northwest of Detroit. He has now done seven barns, all of them in farm country near Detroit, and has three more waiting. Tyler's calling has its problems. The owner of barn C (opposite) withdrew permission in mid-smile. Barn A (above) burned down. Worst of all, Tyler hates working on ladders. Nonetheless, he plans to keep at it. He enjoys putting old masters on the sides of barns; there is always the chance that some passer-by may be amused, or even edified. Most people, for example, know the unfinished work labeled C, but how many others can you identify? Answers below.

Tyler with self-portrait

PHOTOGRAPHED FOR HORIZON BY BALTHAZAR KORAB

A

B

Barn A—*Standing Woman,* by the eighteenth-century Japanese printmaker Kikukawa Eizan; barn B—*Paul Revere,* by John Singleton Copley; barn D—*Baldassare Castiglione,* by Raphael; and barn E—*Federigo da Montefeltro,* by Piero della Francesca

CAN SOCIETY BANISH CRUELTY?

By J. H. PLUMB

No one can doubt that cruelty is a major obscenity of modern life. A woman of eighty is thrown over a railing in Central Park and raped; a small girl is murdered for sexual pleasure; an old man is bayoneted to death for the sake of five dollars. "Snuff films," which progress from mass sex to the deliberate murder and dismemberment of the "actress," are rumored to be displayed in New York City for $200 a seat. Leaving aside the organized violence of war, are we as individuals more cruel than our ancestors? Are we more wanton in our infliction of pain?

In January, 1757, Robert François

Public hanging at Tyburn, 1760

Damiens made a feeble attempt to assassinate Louis XV of France. Though his small knife barely penetrated the king's thick winter clothes, causing little more than a four-inch scratch, Damiens was caught and tortured to make him name his accomplices. He had none. Then he became the centerpiece of a theatre of cruelty. The philosopher La Condamine, for one, was so fascinated by the prospect of such an extravagant spectacle that he got himself a place on the scaffold to watch the victim. He was part of a huge audience that paid exorbitant prices to see Damiens's flesh pulled off with red-hot pincers and his battered

body pulled apart by horses. After that the Parisians—aristocrats, bourgeoisie, and workingmen alike—went back to their dinners.

True, this execution was rather more elaborately staged than most in the eighteenth century, but it was highly traditional. Damiens's executioners had carefully copied, with scrupulous attention to detail, the way François Ravaillac, the assassin of Henry IV, had been put to death in 1610. The French, however, must not be regarded as peculiarly ferocious. The treatment of traitors in England, a method of execution that had first been used against Catholic priests in Queen Elizabeth's reign, was particularly horrifying. Before a vast crowd in a carnival-like atmosphere, the traitor was hanged, but taken down while still alive; then his genitals were cut off and stuffed in his mouth, he was disemboweled, and finally his head was cut off and his trunk quartered. The head, stuck on a pike, would festoon Temple Bar for years; sometimes the quarters were sent to decorate provincial cities.

These were but upsurges in an ocean of cruelty. Several times a year huge crowds swarmed to Tyburn (near Marble Arch in London) to watch and enjoy the executions by hanging of men and

Dutch child swaddled and bound

women, youths and girls, turned off the ladder into eternity for minor robberies and petty pilfering, as well as murder and mayhem. Such sadism was not merely an occasional visual thrill, for

Flogging an underaged laborer

cruelty had been deeply embedded in western European society for centuries and was still to be for a century or so more. It was a constant theme of everyday life, a continuing event of family experience.

Cruelty to animals was widespread—one might say total. Cocks fought each other to the death, bulls and bears were baited by specially trained dogs; cats were sewn up in effigies of the pope to create realistic howls when they were burned. Oxen and horses were driven and flogged until they died. And yet animals were not treated much worse than infants or small children.

The callous behavior of parents and adults to infants in seventeenth-century England or eighteenth-century France is scarcely credible. The women of the poor suckled for a trade, getting as many babies to a meager breast as they could. Naturally their own child was fed first; often the other sucklings were half starved, and frequently hand fed on an appalling diet of pap—a little flour and water. The broken-down hovels to which babies were consigned for wet-nursing were as dirty as they were pitiable. Often there was a dung heap at the door to give warmth, and the floor was strewn with filth of every kind.

Swaddling was universal. Newborn babies were stretched out on a board, a piece of diaper stuck between their thighs, and then were strapped down so tight that they could not move. Swaddled infants were frequently hung up on pegs on the wall and left there, and, of course, they lived in their own feces and urine until they were reswaddled. It is not surprising, therefore, that the death of an infant was an event of small consequence and of exceptional frequency—50 per cent of all infants died before they were a year old.

Childhood was little better. Children were remorselessly flogged. A middle-class child in England was required to stand whenever he was in the presence of his parents and would be savagely punished if he did not. The children of the poor were expected to work as soon as they could walk and were often driven from home to work when little more than seven or eight. Born and bred in a world of callous brutality, the men and women of those days took torture and dismemberment in their stride, were indifferent to the horrors of slavery and the slave trade, and thought nothing of tormenting an idiot or an animal or throwing a witch onto a bonfire.

And then, about 1700, attitudes among the prosperous commercial

Torture on the rack for a dissenter

Hogarth's view: cruelty to animals

classes in England began to change, for reasons that are difficult to comprehend. John Locke protested against swaddling and child beating and argued powerfully that mothers should suckle their own children. Hogarth's satirical prints show that by 1750 hatred of cruelty had a market. Take a long look at his bitter satire *The Four Stages of Cruelty*, in which animals are being flogged to death or tortured, or children casually killed. One print in this series, *Cruelty in Perfection*, depicts a savage and murderous rape. The very fact that Hogarth satirized cruelty shows that there were some flickers of sensitivity to horror.

Men and women formed societies to prevent the worst exploitation of child labor—the young chimney sweeps; they banded together against the slave trade; they helped suppress the most savage type of blood sports. In children's books after 1740, the horrors of cruelty to birds and animals, to fellow human beings, are stressed over and over again. Children were taught to regard cruelty as evil, as sinful. The result was the great wave of humanitarianism that swept Europe and America in the nineteenth century. Wherever we look we find a positive gain over cruelty: public executions largely vanished, torture was stopped. Of course, and this must be stressed, a great tide of cruelty remained, but it was steadily diminishing.

The fight against cruelty was long and arduous; it was largely the campaign of a social and cultural elite whose greatest success may have been in conditioning their own children in the horrors of cruelty. This attitude never permeated the whole of society or restrained the be-

havior of governments. Its influence was always fragile, and in this century cruelty has been widespread and growing toward individuals and toward classes of men and women. True, in previous centuries there would not have been the twentieth-century storms of protest against the more outrageous forms of government cruelty; neither are the worst excesses of personal cruelty allowed to flourish unchecked. But we have no cause to congratulate ourselves, for the position is insecure, and permitting the pornography of violence, which stirs deep and dangerous emotions, is a risk that society can ill afford.

And yet, maybe we should worry more about children's books, which seem singularly devoid of overt morality. Perhaps we are too concerned with the happiness of the child, rather than

Crowd-pleasers in the 1970's: pornography and brutality on film

with the community's happiness with him. Most children are instinctively cruel to animals, and sensitivity toward pain and suffering must be taught. At the same time, the adult world should take a far sterner view of cruelty than it currently does. We need to think clearly about it; we ought to think more carefully about what ought to be forbidden and what not. Surely, there would be no greater folly than to suppress all pornography simply because some of it extols violence. But certainly a good place to start would be the prohibition of *wanton* infliction of pain on another human being.

Skeletons cavort in the Dance of Death in a 1493 woodcut.

THE
BLACK DEATH

It came out of Central Asia,
killing one-third of the European population.
And among the survivors
a new skepticism arose about life and God and
human authority

By PHILIP ZIEGLER

Plague strikes down its victims while fending off the angel Raphael in this detail from a fifteenth-century Italian work. In the complete painting, below, the Virgin Mary shelters the prayerful within the walled city.

In 1346 a Tartar army picked a quarrel with Genoese merchants who traded in the Crimea, chased them into their coastal redoubt at Feodosiya, and laid siege to the town. The usual campaign of attrition was developing when the plans of the attackers were disastrously disrupted by the onslaught of a new and fearful plague. The Tartars abandoned the siege, but not without first sharing their misfortune with their enemies. They used their giant catapults to lob the corpses of the victims over the walls, thus spreading the disease within the city. Though the Genoese carried the rotting bodies through the town and dropped them into the sea, the plague was soon as active within as it was without, for few places are so vulnerable to disease as a besieged city. Those fortunate inhabitants who did not immediately succumb knew quite well that even if they managed to survive the plague, they would be too weak to withstand a renewed Tartar attack. They escaped to their galleys and fled toward the Mediterranean. With them traveled the Black Death. Within three years every third man,

An earthquake devastates a medieval town.

A comet nears the earth.

Locusts descend on crops.

"Knock, Devil, Knock": the plague arrives.

When the plague arrived in Europe, a fearful population, understanding little about contagion, looked back to discover its portents. A major earthquake in Venice, an awe-inspiring comet, a swarm of locusts from Asia in June, 1338—such occurrences, they declared belatedly, should have warned them of the impending disaster.

woman, and child in Europe was dead.

That the Black Death was bubonic plague has been accepted for many years. Bubonic plague is endemic to certain remote areas of the world. From time to time it erupts in minor, localized epidemics. Far more rarely, it surges forth as a great pandemic. Unlike influenza, bubonic plague moves slowly, taking ten years or more to run its course. The high mortality rate of its initial impact is followed by a long period in which it lies endemic, with occasional epidemics that gradually die away in frequency and violence. Finally, perhaps several centuries after the original outbreak, the plague vanishes.

Three such pandemics have been recorded. The first, beginning in Arabia, reached Egypt in 542. It ravaged the Roman Empire of Justinian and moved on across Europe to England, where it was known as the Plague of Cadwalader's Time. The second was that of the Black Death, which died out in the seventeenth century. One of its parting flourishes was the Great Plague of London in 1665. Finally came the pandemic that started in 1892 in Yunnan and reached Bombay in 1896. In India it is believed to have killed some six million people. It moved briefly into Suffolk in 1910, finding only a handful of victims. Quite recently it has made itself felt in

the Azores and parts of South America.

Though it is impossible to be categorical about the origins of the medieval pandemic, recent investigations near Issyk-Kul, a lake in central Asia, show that there was an abnormally high death rate in 1338 and 1339. Memorial stones attribute the deaths to plague. Since this area is in the heart of one of the zones in which bubonic plague lies endemic, it is fairly safe to conclude that this was the cradle of the Black Death. From there it spread eastward into China, south to India, and west to the Crimea some eight years later.

In this fastness of central Asia the bacillus *Pasteurella pestis* has lingered on, living either in the blood stream of an animal or the stomach of a flea. The flea normally favored is *Xenopsylla cheopis*, an insect that, in its turn, usually resides in the hair of some rodent. We will never know for certain what ecological upset began the migration: it could have been flooding, drought, or a sudden increase in the rodent population that strained the available supply of food. Whatever the cause, there is little doubt that infected rats, fleeing from Asia, carried the plague with them to Europe.

The symptoms of bubonic plague as known today coincide precisely with those described by medieval chroniclers.

The bubo is the classic sign. Sometimes this is the size of an almond, sometimes of an orange; it is found in the groin, the armpit, or occasionally on the neck. Equally familiar are the dusky stains or blotches caused by subcutaneous hemorrhaging and the poisoning of the nervous system. Modern doctors, using pain-killing drugs, have found that if the bubo breaks down and suppurates within a week, the victim will probably survive; but few medieval doctors would have expected their patient to endure more than four or five days of the agonizing pain that accompanies the bubo.

Bubonic plague was the first form taken by the Black Death, but a variant known as primary pneumonic, or pulmonary, plague was even more lethal. In the epidemics of the late nineteenth century between 60 and 90 per cent of those who caught bubonic plague died. In the case of pneumonic plague, which attacks the lungs, recovery was virtually unknown. Pneumonic plague also killed more quickly and is perhaps the most infectious of epidemic diseases.

The fourteenth-century plague is unique because in its drive across Europe it changed from pneumonic to bubonic with the seasons of the year. The medieval doctor can hardly be blamed for finding the process incomprehensible. Even if he had under-

HOW THE EPIDEMIC SPREAD

The Black Death originated on the steppes of central Asia, traveling west to reach the Crimea in 1346–47. From there it swept toward Europe, carried aboard ships plying the trade routes of the Black Sea and the Mediterranean. After the plague arrived in Messina, Sicily, early in October, 1347, it moved rapidly across the Continent, blanketing the British Isles by the end of 1349 and Scandinavia by December, 1350. Curiously, certain towns like Liège were untouched by the Black Death, and a large part of central eastern Europe escaped altogether. Why such regions were less susceptible is unknown to modern historians.

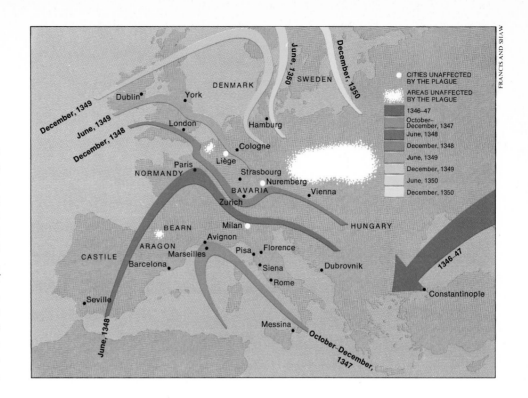

stood it, he would not have mastered the full story. For there were also cases in which a man would die within a few hours or go to bed in the best of health and never wake up.

The third element in the Black Death, septicemic plague, was here at work. This, like bubonic plague, is transmitted by insects. The brunt of the infection falls on the blood stream, which, within an hour or two, is swarming with plague bacilli. The victim is dead long before buboes have formed. In this variety of plague, a man-borne flea, *Pulex irritans*, has a chance to operate. So rich in bacilli is the blood of a sick man that the flea can easily become infected and carry the disease to a new victim. Septicemic plague must have been the rarest of the three interwoven diseases that made up the Black Death, but it was certainly as lethal as its pneumonic cousin.

The population that awaited the Black Death in Europe was ill equipped to resist it. The medieval peasant—distracted by war, weakened by malnutrition, exhausted by his struggle to win a living from his inadequate portion of ever less fertile land—was physically an easy prey for the disease. Intellectually and emotionally, he was prepared for disaster and ready to accept it if not actually welcome it.

The Europeans of the fourteenth cen-

tury were convinced that the plague was an affliction laid on them by the Almighty, a retribution for the wickedness of the present generation. Credulous and superstitious, they believed without question in the direct participation of God on earth and were well versed in Old Testament precedents for the destruction of cities or whole races in an access of divine indignation. Because they were unable to see a natural explanation of this sudden holocaust, they took it for granted that they were the victims of God's wrath.

Given so grim a sense of destiny, it is to the credit of the medieval physicians that they devoted themselves to preventing or curing the infection. It is, however, hardly surprising that their efforts proved inadequate. Sudhoff's great archives of medical history, published in Germany in 1925, reproduce more than two hundred and eighty plague treatises; seventy-seven were written before 1400 and at least twenty before 1353. There is much windy nothingness in these, but also a certain amount of common sense and sound judgment. Certainly there was a depressing readiness to stress that flight or prayer was the only possible defense, but the patient was also given some guidance on how he should conduct himself.

There were frequent differences of opinion among the experts. Simon of Covino thought pregnant women and "those of fragile nature," like undernourished paupers, would be the first to go—a conclusion the Medical Faculty of Paris rejected, claiming that those "whose bodies are replete with humors" were the most vulnerable. There was more agreement on the best place to live. Seclusion was the first priority. After that, the problem was how to avoid the infected air that carried death from land to land. A low site, sheltered from the wind, was desirable. The coast was to be shunned because of the corrupt mists that were creeping across the surface of the sea. Houses should be built facing north, and windows should be glazed or covered with waxed cloth.

If the infection was carried by corrupted air, something was needed to build up antibodies. Anything aromatic was considered of value. For example, it was good to burn dry and richly scented woods, like juniper, ash, vine, or rosemary. Diet was important, too. Fish from the infected waters of the sea was prohibited, but eggs were authorized if eaten with vinegar.

It was bad to sleep by day and best to keep the heat of the liver steady by sleeping first on the right side and then on the left. To sleep on one's back was disas-

Pope Gregory the Great leads a litany procession in Rome in 590, praying for an end to the first pandemic plague. This miniature from the Très Riches Heures *of the duc de Berry was painted by Pol Limburg, whose brothers, Hermann and Jan, witnessed similar proceedings in Paris during the Black Death.*

trous, since this would cause a stream of superfluities to descend on the palate and nostrils. These would flow to the brain and submerge the memory.

Bad drove out bad, and to imbibe foul odors was a useful protection. According to another contemporary writer, John Colle: "Attendants who take care of latrines are nearly all to be considered immune." It was not unknown for apprehensive citizens to spend hours each day crouched over a latrine absorbing the fetid smells.

These were mainly preventives; once the disease struck, the remedies became still more irrelevant. Bleeding was a part of almost every treatment: if the patient fainted, wrote one physician heartlessly, pour cold water over him and continue as before. Various soothing potions were prescribed, in particular, a blend of apple syrup, lemon, rose water, and peppermint. This became less agreeable when powdered minerals were added to the mixture. There was some belief in the virtues of emeralds and pearls, and the medicinal qualities of gold were taken for granted. One recipe instructed: take an ounce of best gold, add eleven ounces of quicksilver, dissolve by slow heat, let the quicksilver escape, add forty-seven ounces of water of borage, keep airtight for three days over a fire, and drink until cured, or, as was more probable, death supervened. At least the high price of gold insured that not many invalids could be thus poisoned.

Most fourteenth-century people regarded their doctor with tolerance and respect but also with an uncomfortable conviction that he was irrelevant to the real problems of their lives. They were, of course, ready to believe almost anything that was told them with authority, but their faith had been considerably undermined by the doctor's own lack of confidence. Resignation or anguished fear was the only reaction his activities could reasonably inspire.

The Black Death arrived in Messina, Sicily, early in October, 1347. Within a few days the plague had taken a firm grasp. Too late to save themselves, the citizens turned on the sailors who had brought them this disastrous cargo and drove them from the port. With their departure, the Black Death was scattered around the Mediterranean, but Messina's sufferings were no lighter for its dispersion. With hundreds of victims dying every day, the population panicked. They fled from their doomed city into the fields of southern Sicily, seeking safety in isolation and carrying the plague with them through the countryside.

From Sicily the plague spread probably to north Africa by way of Tunis; certainly to Corsica and Sardinia; to the Balearics and Almería, Valencia, and Barcelona on the Iberian peninsula; and to southern Italy. The disease closely followed the main trade routes: whether the Black Death traveled by rat, unescorted flea, or infected sailor, a ship was the surest means, and its first targets were the coastal towns. It traveled from the Crimea to Moscow, not overland, but by way of Italy, France, England, and the Hanseatic ports.

The three great centers for the propagation of the plague in southern Europe were Sicily, Genoa, and Venice. It seems to have arrived at the latter ports some time in January, 1348. But it was Pisa, a few weeks later, that provided the main point of entry to central and northern Italy. From there it moved inland to Rome and Tuscany. It had begun the march that would not end until the whole of the European continent had been blanketed by death.

France was the next country to be overrun. The plague arrived at Marseilles a month or two after it reached the mainland of Italy. Through 1348 it moved across the country, advancing on two main lines, toward Bordeaux in the west and Paris in the north. The fate of Perpignan illustrates vividly what happened in many of the smaller cities. The disruption of everyday commercial life is shown by statistics of loans made by the Jews of Perpignan to their Christian co-citizens. In January, 1348, there were sixteen such loans, in February, twenty-five, in March, thirty-two. There were eight in the first eleven days of April,

A bedside consultation

Russian cross

Herbalist's jar

Hazelnut amulet

Curing by cupping

Protective garb for a doctor

Medieval doctors knew nothing about the causes of the plague, and little about possible cures. With primitive medicines and techniques, like the process of cupping to remove "infected" blood, and a large dose of superstition—crosses and amulets were popular—they attempted to give relief to the victims. Hoping to gain immunity, they often wore costumes like the one above: the beak of the mask held spices that "purified" the air, while the wand was used to determine the victim's pulse from a distance.

Riddled with arrows that symbolize pestilence, Saint Sebastian (at top) intercedes with Christ to spare the inhabitants of a Provençal town. In the foreground of the painting, a priest reads the burial service over shrouded victims while one gravedigger himself succumbs to the disease.

three in the rest of the month, and then no more until August 12. Of 125 scribes and legists known to have been active shortly before the Black Death, only forty-five survived. Physicians fared even worse—only one out of eight survived —while sixteen out of eighteen barber-surgeons perished or, at least, disappeared. In Avignon, then the papal capital, Pope Clement VI retreated to his chamber, saw nobody, and spent day and night sheltering between two enormous fires. He survived, but Petrarch's beloved Laura died in the same town.

Germany is of peculiar interest since it provided the setting for two of the Black Death's most unpleasant by-products. The first was the Flagellant movement. The Brotherhood of the Flagellants, or Brethren of the Cross, as the movement was called in 1348, traditionally originated in eastern Europe, but it was in Germany that it really took root, and it was the Black Death that turned the whim of a freakish minority into a powerful international force. The Flagellants marched in long processions, two by two. Men and women were segregated, the women taking their place toward the rear. At the head was the group master. Except for occasional hymns the marchers were silent, their heads and faces hidden in cowls, their eyes fixed on the ground. They were dressed in somber clothes with red crosses on the back and front.

At the news that the Brethren of the Cross were on the way, the townsfolk would pour out to welcome them. The first move was to the church, where they would chant their special litany. The real business, however, usually took place outside. A circle was formed and the worshipers stripped to the waist. Their outer garments were piled inside the circle, and the sick of the village would congregate there in the hope of acquiring a little vicarious merit.

First the master thrashed those who had committed offenses against the order, then came the collective flagellation. Each brother carried a heavy scourge with three or four leather thongs, the thongs tipped with metal studs. With those they began rhythmically to beat their backs and breasts. Three of the brethren, acting as cheerleaders, led the ceremonies. The worshipers kept up the tempo and their spirits by chanting the hymn of the Flagellants. The pace grew. Each man tried to outdo his neighbor, literally whipping himself into a frenzy. Around them the townsfolk quaked, sobbed, and groaned in sympathy.

Such activities might seem harmless, but the movement became less reputable and was taken over by a small group who used their power to bully and blackmail the local inhabitants. One can understand and forgive much because of the panic that impelled these misguided fanatics, but it is impossible to condone the impulse they gave to the second strange by-product of the Black Death, the persecution of the Jews.

It was perhaps inevitable that a people overwhelmed by fear and suffering should seek revenge. The Jews were not the only candidates. In Spain the Arabs, in France the English, in England the lepers—all were at one time suspected of spreading the plague. But there were also economic reasons for wanting the Jews out of the way, and these, allied with traditional anti-Semitism, ripened into a ferocious conviction that the Jews were poisoning the wells. The first cases occurred in the south of France, but the madness might never have spread if, at a trial at Chillon in September, 1348, lurid confessions of guilt had not been racked from certain of the accused. This settled the doubts or perhaps quieted the consciences of many who might otherwise have felt bound to protect the Jews. The municipality of Zurich voted never to admit them to the city again. In Basel the Jews were penned up in wooden buildings and burned alive.

"In November began the persecution of the Jews," wrote a German chronicler. In that month Jews were burned at Solothurn, Zofingen, and Stuttgart; in December at Landsberg, Burren, Memmingen, Lindau; in January at Fribourg and Ulm. Gotha and Dresden followed, and at Speyer bodies of the murdered were piled in great wine casks and sent floating down the Rhine. A lull of a few months ended in fresh outbreaks extending to Spain and Flanders. The persecution of the Jews waned only with the plague itself. It is a curious reflection on human nature that the European, overwhelmed by what was probably the greatest natural calamity ever to strike his continent, reacted by rivaling the cruelty of nature in the hideousness of his own man-made atrocities.

That the persecution of the Jews did not accompany the Black Death to England owes less to superior tolerance than to the fact that almost all of them had already been expelled. The first cases of the plague probably occurred at

To help stave off the plague, many prayed to Saint Roch, above, who had ministered to its victims and died of the disease.

Melcombe Regis, in Dorset, in June or July of 1348. By the end of 1349 the British Isles had been blanketed.

England, saved from foreign invasion and relatively unscathed by civil war, is peculiarly rich in archives that illustrate vividly and in detail the life of the past. The ecclesiastical books of institutions and patent rolls, the memorial court rolls and account rolls provide material to plot the course of the Black Death with greater authority than elsewhere in Europe. Inevitably we know most about the clergy. It might be supposed that the beneficed clergy, with their education,

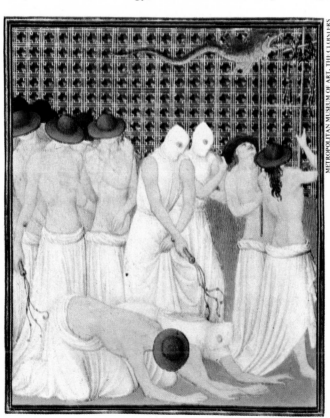

In an excess of emotionalism, and in the hope that self-mortification would render them immune to the dread plague, members of the Flagellant movement receive a lashing from two white-hooded masters in this miniature from the Belles Heures *of Jean, duc de Berry.*

high standard of living, and less cramped living quarters, would be better placed to survive than their unfortunate flocks. But, on the whole, the arguments that suggest a higher death rate among priests are more convincing. Their work, if conscientiously carried out, brought them into constant contact with the infected; their average age was relatively high; and their smaller households, though less easily infected, were more vulnerable once penetrated. One rat family to a household and three fleas to a rat seems to have been the norm; the greater the number of infected fleas in proportion to potential human victims, the smaller were the chances of escape.

What is certain is that the clergy suffered hideously. It is extraordinary to note when visiting medieval churches how often the incumbent was replaced once, twice, or even three times during the plague. In Bristol, for example, ten out of eighteen clergymen died. Not that the laity did much better. The Little Red Book of Bristol lists the names of the town council, the "forty-eight," for 1349. Of the fifty-two members that the "forty-eight" whimsically contained, the names of fifteen had been struck through. If all these died of the plague, the mortality rate would have been slightly under 30 per cent, unusually high for the cream of the city dignitaries. Things were far worse in the crowded and stinking warrens in which the poor were forced to live. "The plague," according to an old calendar, "raged to such a degree that the living were scarce able to bury the dead . . . the grass grew several inches high in the High Street."

The Black Death reached London early in 1349. The existing graveyards were soon too small to meet the demand. A new cemetery was opened at Smithfield, while the distinguished soldier and courtier Sir Walter de Manny bought some thirteen acres of unused

Plague-ridden communities sought desperately for scapegoats, and Jews were relentlessly persecuted during the fourteenth century. Those above, in a woodcut from a German chronicle, are being burned en masse.

land to the northwest of the city at Spittle Croft. He built a chapel, dedicated to the Annunciation, and threw it open for the overflow of victims. The London historian John Stow recorded an inscription in the churchyard that read: "A great plague raging in the year of our Lord 1349, this churchyard was consecrated; wherein, and within the bounds of the present monastery, were buried more than fifty thousand bodies of the dead . . . whose souls God have mercy upon. Amen."

A figure of fifty thousand for a city of sixty or seventy thousand inhabitants must be nonsensical. Statistics for the big cities are particularly hard to establish, but it seems more probable that between twenty and thirty thousand died—a sufficiently terrifying figure to satisfy even the most bloodthirsty chronicler.

London survived. In 1377 its population was only about thirty-five thousand, but this was after further attacks of plague. The fact that all the chancery and exchequer work continued to be done there was a powerful magnet, and there was no English city in which an escaping villein could conceal himself with greater confidence. Within a few years much of the lost ground was probably made up.

Yet the mark left by the Black Death was seen not only in the cemeteries. The sharp fall in moral standards, noticed in so many parts of Europe at this period, was nowhere more striking than in London. Criminals flocked into the city, and chroniclers tell of the great increase in lawbreaking. After this period, the city

began to enjoy a dubious reputation for wealth and for wickedness. Thomas Walsingham denounced the Londoners roundly: "They were of all people the most proud, arrogant and greedy, disbelieving in God, disbelieving in ancient custom." Those who live in great cities are traditionally believed to be harder, more sophisticated, and more rapacious than their country cousins, but the Londoner probably deserved his reputation. Yet a city that suffers as London suffered, and rebounds rapidly to even greater prosperity, can perhaps be excused a certain fall from grace during the years of its recovery.

In London thirty thousand out of seventy thousand died. Was this true of England as a whole, of France and Italy? Statistics are always hazardous, in the Middle Ages particularly so. All one can do is extrapolate from the small pockets of certain knowledge—the lists of beneficed clergy, court rolls for certain manors, post-mortems—and venture a guess. In spite of the limitations of such methods, one can arrive with some confidence at an approximate conclusion. The statement that a third of the population of Europe died of the Black Death should not be too misleading. The figure might quite easily be as high as 40 per cent or as low as 30 per cent; it could conceivably be as high as 45 per cent or as low as 25 per cent. These are surely the outside limits.

One-third of a continent's population cannot be so abruptly eliminated without considerable dislocation to its economy and social structure. The historian must expect to find conspicuous changes in the life of the European community immediately following the Black Death. Some traces of the scars will survive into the succeeding decades or even centuries. But exactly what these changes were has been the subject of bitter and protracted debate.

It is unquestioned that, in England at least, the Black Death did not so much introduce radical changes as vastly accelerate changes already going on. England had already begun to move from the manorial system by which the villein

Death, ever present, rides a skeletal pale horse

...his fresco by an unknown Dutch artist. The personification of Death, and its inevitable triumph, was a persistent theme in art throughout the time of the plague.

held his land in return for services rendered to a new relationship in which land was rented and services paid for in cash. The sudden disappearance of so much of the labor force meant that those who already worked for wages were able to demand an increase, while the rest clamored to share in the freemen's privilege. If the landlord refused, conditions were peculiarly propitious for the villein to slip away and seek a more amenable master elsewhere. As successive waves of the pandemic broke over the countryside, the balance between tenant and landlord swung still farther. Wages in many areas more or less doubled, prices temporarily fell, labor grew more mobile. Inevitably there was a backlash. Though the genesis of the Peasant's Revolt of 1381 may be found far earlier, it was the Black Death that ultimately created the conditions in which rebellion became inevitable.

The pattern of centuries was breaking up; not only the pattern of society but of men's minds as well. Any account of the Black Death that ignored its impact on the minds of its victims would be notably incomplete. Its effects endured. Within only a few years the horrors of the plague had been thrust from the forefront of people's minds, but certainly no one can live through a catastrophe so devastating without retaining the psychic scars forever.

People felt, fairly or unfairly, that the Church had let them down. It had failed to protect its flock, had forfeited its claim to special status. On the whole the best of the churchmen perished; those who shirked their duty survived to preach again. In 1351 Pope Clement VI accused his clergy of arrogance, covetousness, and licentious living: in so doing he spoke for the majority of mankind.

The decades that followed the plague saw not only a decline in the spiritual authority of the Church but also a growth of religious fervor. There was a spate of church building throughout Europe. In Italy, nearly fifty new religious holidays were created. The number of pilgrims to Rome and other centers remained con-

A PRIMER ON PLAGUES

Rattus rattus

Although most Americans would say it could never happen here, the plague does exist in the United States. In 1975 there were twenty reported cases, the largest number since 1924. The plague is a zoonosis, a disease that can be transmitted from animal to animal and from animal to man. In the fourteenth-century plague, the bacillus *Pasteurella pestis* was carried primarily by a rodent-borne flea, *Xenopsylla cheopis*. It was first an endemic, a disease confined to one locality. As it gathered force, it became an epidemic, spreading throughout a larger region, and then a pandemic, afflicting people over a wide geographic area. Other pandemics have occurred since then, one of the most devastating of them

Xenopsylla cheopis

within our own century. In the influenza pandemic of 1918–19, three waves swept the world, killing at least 20 million people, 548,000 in the United States alone. Experts suspect that the deadly strain may have been akin to the swine influenza virus recently found at Fort Dix, New Jersey, but no one will ever know for sure. Flu viruses were not finally isolated until the 1930's, more than a decade after the so-called Spanish influenza, unchecked by vaccines or antibiotics, had taken its fearful toll.

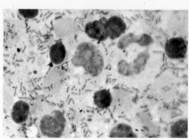

Pasteurella pestis

stant or increased, even though a third of those who might have made the journey were now dead. The second half of the fourteenth century was marked by resentment at the wealth and complacency of the Church and by fundamental questioning of its philosophy and its organization. In England it was the age of Wycliffe and of Lollardry, a new and aggressive anticlericalism. In Italy it was the great period of the Fraticelli, dissident Franciscans who believed that poverty was the essence of Christ. The second half of the fourteenth century was a time of spiritual unrest, of disrespect for established idols and a search for strange gods. In the end the Reformation would have happened anyway, but the tempo would have been slower, opposition more intense, reaction more immoderate.

Faith disappeared, or was transformed: men became at once sceptical and intolerant. It is not at all the modern, serenely cold, and imperturbable scepticism; it is a violent movement of the whole nature which feels itself impelled to burn what it adores; but the man is uncertain in his doubt, and his burst of laughter stuns him; he has passed, as it were, through an orgy, and when the white light of the morning comes he will have an attack of despair, profound anguish with tears and perhaps a vow of pilgrimage and a conspicuous conversion.

J. J. Jusserand's classic description of the European in the second half of the fourteenth century captures admirably the twin elements of skepticism and timorous uncertainty. The generation that survived the plague could not believe, but did not dare deny. It groped toward the future, with one nervous eye always peering over its shoulder toward the past. Neurotic gloom is a state of mind not wholly unknown in the West today. We are closer in spirit to our medieval ancestors than our parents or grandparents ever were. We can, at least, take some comfort from the fact that they survived.

Philip Ziegler, an Englishman, writes history as an amateur—from amāre, *to love. He recently wrote a book on William IV.*

Grateful parishioners in the town of Plougastel-Daoulas, France, built the monument opposite in 1602–1604 to commemorate the end of the plague.

The Odd Couple

A latter-day neighbor
of Jane and Thomas Carlyle describes
the goings on
in this Victorian household

Thomas Carlyle, age seventy-eight

Jane Welsh Carlyle, age fifty-three

Marriage is described in the Anglican prayer book as an "excellent mystery"; and this phrase (though I understand, of course, that the word "mystery" had a somewhat different meaning for a sixteenth-century bishop) has always stimulated my imagination. Every marriage is slightly mysterious, whether the partnership succeeds or fails, and as a literary biographer I am again and again confronted by the problems of my subject's married life. Usually there is something about it that I find I cannot quite analyze; but I have found no marriage quite so strange as the long, devoted, inharmonious alliance of Jane and Thomas Carlyle.

Solemnized in October, 1826, it lasted until 1866, and before they plighted their troth, both husband and wife had expressed the deepest hesitations. "Without great sacrifices on both sides," Carlyle had written, "the possibility of our union is an empty dream"; while Jane had declared in 1823, "Your Friend I will be . . . but your Wife! Never, never!"

To some extent the obstacle they confronted was social and economic. Jane was "an ex-spoilt child," brought up by an adoring mother in Scottish middle-class society, well educated, attractive, equally proud, we are told, of her Latin and her eyelashes; whereas Carlyle's father was a rustic stonemason who had later taken up farming. Thomas had made himself a historian and a writer by dint of his own laborious efforts, but in the process he had ruined his health and suffered perpetually from dyspepsia, insomnia, and a host of nerv-

ous ills. Jane admired him, but felt that she could not love him.

Yet the rough peasant-scholar and the volatile middle-class girl had somehow drifted into marriage, and as a middle-aged woman, Jane would write to a favorite cousin, explaining what she thought had happened: "In virtue of his being *the least unlikable* man in the place, I let him dance attendance on my young person, till I came to *need* him— all the same as my slippers to go to a ball in, or my bonnet to go out to walk. When I finally agreed to marry him, I *cried* excessively and felt excessively shocked—but if I had then said *no* he would have left me."

For the first few years of their marriage, she accepted the consequences of her decision bravely. In 1828 they moved from Edinburgh to the lonely farm of Craigenputtock, where the silence was so profound that they could often hear sheep cropping in the field outside. During the winter months, a deeper hush descended, and the snow piled up against the door: when they opened it, a mountainous drift would sweep like an avalanche across the flagstones of the kitchen.

Finally, in 1834, Carlyle having at last published *Sartor Resartus*, they felt rich enough to move south. The London house they chose was Number 5 Great Cheyne Row (today Number 24 Cheyne Row), a largish Queen Anne house close to the river Thames, which at that period still retained the muddy foreshore that Whistler and Walter Greaves painted, where barges and sailing boats lay beached on its verge, amid decrepit wharves and ramshackle wooden jetties. They were to spend the rest of their lives in that house. There Jane Carlyle's body was brought after her sudden death in 1866; and there, an embittered, disconsolate sage, Carlyle died in 1881.

For me the long years they spent at Cheyne Row have a special interest. I am their next-door neighbor, and rarely a day passes when I am not somehow reminded of them. Chelsea itself has changed. It is no longer a secluded suburb, full of trees and ancient houses;

By PETER QUENNELL

With Jane's dog, Nero, beside him, Thomas Carlyle smokes a pipe in the garden behind Number 5 Great Cheyne Row on a summer evening in 1857.

late-Victorian buildings have swamped the "hawthorn lanes," meadows, and market gardens that once extended beyond the King's Road toward Kensington and Knightsbridge.

Yet Cheyne Row keeps much of its quietude, and the Carlyles' house (now a literary museum) preserves its cloistral, somewhat gloomy atmosphere. Most of the changes it has undergone since it was erected in the year 1708—by a speculative builder who had bought up the bowling green of a demolished manor house—were made by the Carlyles themselves. Jane was no respecter of early eighteenth-century paneling. Perhaps because she liked to think of herself as modern, or because she identified the depression that Carlyle frequently radiated with the somber background of their old-fashioned house, or perhaps because she dreaded the bugs that often hid behind antique woodwork, she removed the paneling from many walls and substituted, if she could afford it, prettily flowered wallpaper.

From Number 26 Cheyne Row, our view of the Carlyles' house is particularly absorbing. Just below, as we look to the right across an antiquated redbrick wall, lies the strip of garden where Carlyle, on summer evenings, used to smoke his clay pipe, which he stored in a crevice between the bricks. The photograph on page 99, taken in 1857, shows him seated near the garden door, wearing the tall-crowned, large-brimmed black hat that shadowed his then gray-bearded visage; little Nero, Jane's dog, is comfortably spread-eagled beside his chair. Nero, who is buried in the garden, was an important member of the Carlyle household and appears in a series of dramatic tales. There was one occasion, Jane relates, when the intrepid animal tried to fly:

For a first attempt his success was not so bad . . . and tho' he *did* plash down on the pavement at the feet of an astonished Boy he broke no bones, was only quite *stunned*. . . . It was after breakfast, and he had been standing at the open window, watching the birds—one of his chief delights—while Elizabeth was "dusting out" for Mr. C. Lying in my bed, I heard thro' the deal partition Elizabeth scream; "oh God! oh Nero!" and rush downstairs like a strong wind out at the street door. I sat up in my bed aghast—waiting with a feeling as of the Heavens falling till I heard her reascending the stairs and then I sprang to meet her in my night shift. She was white as a sheet, ready to faint. . . . "Is he killed?" I asked. . . . Mr. C. came down from his bedroom with his chin all over soap and asked, "has anything happened to Nero?" "Oh Sir he *must* have broken *all* his legs, he leapt out at *your* window!"

"God bless me!" said Mr. C. and returned to finish his shaving.

His mistress adored him, and his master valued his company. Nero regularly followed Carlyle on his long crepuscular walks through Chelsea—"little dim-white speck of Life, of Love, Fidelity and Feeling; girdled by the Darkness of Night Eternal"—while the sage meditated, as he trudged the streets, upon the evils of the modern world and his own forlorn existence, or thought of the sleepless hours that awaited him once he had plodded back to his solitary bed.

In the same photograph, a clump of bushes and a small tree occupy the right-hand side. They conceal a homely domestic office. From our upper windows we look down upon a modest flat-roofed structure. This is the household privy. The Carlyles, while they occupied Number 5, had no kind of interior sanitation; and as both of them seem to have suffered from perpetually disordered livers, and Carlyle was constantly being dispatched to the chemist's shop in search of the powerful laxative called "blue pills," the fact that they had only an unheated outdoor privy on wet and windy London days must have caused them much acute discomfort.

Another odd thought is how many of the Carlyles' troubles originated in the

---

Pursuit by Post

On June 4, 1821, four days after his introduction to Jane Baillie Welsh, Thomas Carlyle wrote her a long letter, concluding: "It seems as if we had known each other from infancy upwards. . . ." This was the beginning of a correspondence that was to last until Jane's death in April, 1866. Frustrated in her own literary ambitions (others besides Dickens declared she was a born novelist), Jane revealed her wit and personality in the thousands of letters she wrote—to Carlyle during their five-year courtship and their forty years of marriage, to her family, to her friends. She was intelligent, sensitive, self-aware, waspish at times, and remarkably strong-willed.

Carlyle came to know these aspects of Jane well during their courtship, which was conducted almost entirely by mail (indeed, the volume of letters exchanged suggests that the couple were so busy writing to each other they had no time to get married). At first the correspondence was primarily intellectual in tone, for Carlyle had undertaken to improve Miss Welsh's mind. Yet he cannot have overlooked her charms, for as early as January, 1822, she was obliged to send him this withering rebuke:

"I have moreover read your Letter. For *it* I do *not* thank you. . . . there is about your Letter a *mystery* which I detest. It is so full of *meaning* words underlined; *meaning* sentences half-finished; *meaning* blanks with notes of admiration; and *meaning* quotations from foreign languages, that really in this abundance of meaning it seems to indicate, I am somewhat at a loss to discover what you would be at. . . . Now Sir, once for all, I beg you to understand that I dislike as much as my Mother disapproves your somewhat too ardent expressions of Friendship toward me; and that if you cannot write to me as to a man who feels a deep interest in your welfare, who admires your talents, respects your virtues, and for the sake of these has often,—perhaps too

house we now inhabit. For them it was an almost legendary place, peopled by a series of demonic families whose principal purpose, so far as Jane could make out, was to prevent Carlyle from writing. The earliest, a rather genteel family called Lambert, arrived in 1839. With them, alas, they had brought a parrot, which, when they carried it into the garden, screeched under Carlyle's window, so that he "fairly sprang to his feet, declaring he could 'neither think nor live.'" Jane then composed a diplomatic note, and the parrot was removed.

Worse came when one of the Misses Lambert started taking music lessons, both vocal and instrumental. Carlyle was working then on the first floor, and only a thin wall divided him from the sitting room—it is still our sitting room—that the Misses Lambert used. His patience was limited; his hatred of any kind of noise had already developed into an obsession; and one morning he suddenly left his table, seized the poker, and delivered a couple of tremendous blows on the wall "exactly opposite where he fancied the young Lady seated." The deep silence that followed

Today Great Cheyne Row is merely Cheyne Row, but the Carlyle house (third from the left) remains almost exactly as Thomas Carlyle knew it before he died in 1881. Our author lives next door to the left.

lasted "for the next twelve hours." But neither this drastic action nor a polite exchange of notes could quite subdue the Misses Lambert, and intermittent "squallings" and tinklings continued to torment Carlyle—he was then toiling at *Past and Present* and his monumental book on Oliver Cromwell—throughout 1842 and 1843.

Even worse than the musical Lamberts were some of the families who succeeded them—the Roncas, a bohemian Irish family who, besides noisily carpentering in the back garden and hanging out their squalid household laundry, kept a parrot, dogs, and chickens. After much diplomacy and some stern threats, they were at last reduced to order. But

then in 1865, the year before Jane's death, another fearful blow descended. The latest tenant, "a very mysterious 'dressmaker,'" seemed a retiring, inoffensive person. But she had lodgers who proved to be more troublesome, and early one morning Mrs. Carlyle made a hideous discovery. As she wrote in a letter on December 25:

For years back there has reigned over all these gardens a heavenly quiet—thanks to my heroic exertions in exterminating nuisances. . . . Figure then my horror, my despair, on being waked one dark morning with the crowing of a cock, that seemed to issue from under my bed! . . . I lay with my heart in my mouth . . . listening for Mr. C.'s foot stamping frantically, as of old. . . . So soon as it was daylight I looked out . . . and there was a sight to see—a ragged, *irish*-looking hen house . . . and sauntering to and fro nine goodly hens, and a stunning cock!

Once again she managed to intervene and arranged "that the cock should be shut up in a cellar . . . from three in the afternoon till ten in the morning," by which time Mr. C. would have retired to the dismal soundproof room that he had now had built on the top floor. Jane,

---

often, overlooked your faults;—if you cannot write to me as if—as if you were married, you need never waste ink or paper on me more. . . ."

Carlyle at once replied that his feelings toward Jane were "those of an honest man and a true-hearted friend," and there the matter rested for quite some time. But it had inaugurated a theme that was to pervade their early letters: he hinting at a more intimate future together, she shrinking from his literary advances. In one notable exchange, Carlyle wrote on August 31, 1823:

"Alas! my fate is dreary and obscure and perilous: is it fit that you . . . whom I love more dearly than my own soul, should partake in it? . . . The only thing I know is that you are the most delightful, enthusiastic, contemptuous, affectionate, sarcastic, capricious, warm-hearted, lofty-minded, half-devil, half-angel of a woman that ever ruled over the heart of a man; that I will love you, must love you, whatever may betide, till the last moment of my existence; and that if we both act rightly our lot *may* be the happiest of a thousand mortal lots. So let us cling to one another . . . forever and ever!"

Jane answered almost immediately, on September 16:

"You misunderstand me. You regard me no longer as a Friend, a Sister, but as one who at some future period may be more to you than

both. . . . And, my God! what have I said or done to mislead you into an error so destructive to the confidence that subsists betwixt us, so dangerous to the peace of both? . . . it is of no use talking of what I might or should have done in the time past. I have only to repair the mischief in as far as I can, now that my eyes are opened to it, now that I am startled to find our relation actually assuming the aspect of an engagement for life.

"My Friend, I love you. . . . But were you my Brother I would love you the same; were I married to another I would love you the same. And is this sentiment so calm, so delightful, but so unimpassioned, enough to recompense the freedom of my heart, enough to reconcile me to the existence of a married woman, the hopes and wishes and ambitions of which are all so different from mine, the cares and occupations of which are my disgust! Oh no! Your Friend I will be, your truest most devoted Friend, while I breathe the breath of life; but your Wife! Never, never! not though you were as rich as Croesus, as honoured and as renowned as you yet shall be."

Carlyle, undaunted, did not abandon his suit. As the years went by, and the letters went back and forth, Jane was gradually won over. On October 3, 1826, she wrote to him, "Oh, my dearest Friend! be always *so* good to me, and I shall make the best and happiest Wife." Two weeks later, Jane Baillie Welsh and Thomas Carlyle were married.

whose character evidently included a certain touch of masochism, must somehow have relished such domestic dramas. She had thought of writing a novel, she admitted, about the "mysteries" of Number 6, and used to amuse her friend Charles Dickens with the curious stories she told him of the house and its inhabitants. Dickens believed that they would make an excellent book. He had always admired her gifts—"none of the writing women came near her at all," he said, and as a man who enjoyed the companionship of the opposite sex, he found her more than usually attractive. Not only, noted his biographer John Forster, did Mrs. Carlyle entertain him, she inspired a deeper sentiment: "there was something beyond, beyond"—an element of physical and emotional sympathy.

Indeed, long after she had lost her looks and had become elderly and gaunt and haggard, Jane was still charming, and many of the distinguished men who presented themselves at Number 5 Cheyne Row arrived to visit Jane alone. Both the Italian patriot Giuseppe Mazzini and the French exile Godefroy Cavaignac (one of the leaders of the left wing under Charles X and Louis Philippe) had undoubtedly conceived a romantic affection for their hostess, and their love was, to some extent, returned. She also had the adoration of the aging Leigh Hunt, who, with his untidy children and his feckless and difficult wife, lived in Upper Cheyne Row around the corner.

Marianne Hunt, whom Byron had once so cordially detested, had apparently taken to the bottle, and the Hunts led an improvident and harassed existence. Hunt—"a pretty man," Carlyle remembered, "... with the airiest kindly style of sparkling talk"— often took refuge at Number 5 from the squalid confusion of his own home. "He would lean on his elbow against the mantelpiece ... and look around him ... before taking leave for the night: 'as if I were a *Lar*,' said he once, 'or permanent Household God here!'... Another time, rising from this

Leigh Hunt *Geraldine Jewsbury*

Giuseppe Mazzini *Harriet Martineau*

During their forty years together, Jane and Thomas each maintained warm friendships outside their marriage. The poet Leigh Hunt and the Italian patriot Giuseppe Mazzini admired and comforted Jane, while the novelist Geraldine Jewsbury and the economist Harriet Martineau doted upon Thomas Carlyle.

Lar attitude, he repeated (voice very fine) as if in sport of parody, yet with something of very sad perceptible: 'While I to sulphurous and penal fire'—as the last thing before vanishing." Among Hunt's best-known poems is the graceful triolet "Jenny Kissed Me," which he addressed to Jane when she had surprised him by jumping from her chair to throw her arms around him as he entered.

Both the Carlyles, despite their quirks and prejudices, were fond of entertaining newcomers. Since the publication of *Sartor Resartus*, Carlyle had become a literary lion, and Jane, for all her caustic asides, was pleased to see "the host of my husband's lady admirers" gathered about him in her presence. There was Harriet Martineau, the famous political economist, holding out her ear trumpet "with a pretty blushing air of coquetry," and later, the novelist Geraldine Jewsbury, lying on the carpet at the great man's feet.

Nor were the Carlyles averse to fashionable society, though Jane often criticized its arrogance and extravagance. She records in a letter to her mother, written on April 7, 1839, that a week previously "the sound of a whirlwind

rushed thro' the street, and there stopt with a prancing of steeds and footman thunder at this door, an equipage, all resplendent with sky-blue and silver . . . whence emanated Count d'Orsay." The renowned exquisite had behaved in a particularly gracious manner, while his host, never easy to impress, had displayed a solid homespun dignity:

A sight it was to make one think the millennium actually at hand, when the lion and the lamb, and all incompatible things should consort together. Carlyle in his grey plaid suit . . . looking blandly at the Prince of Dandies; and the Prince of Dandies on an opposite chair, all resplendent as a diamond-beetle, looking blandly at *him*. D'Orsay is a really handsome man, after one has heard him speak and found that he has both wit and sense; but at first sight his beauty is of that rather disgusting sort which seems to be like genius "of no sex." And this impression is greatly helped by the fantastical finery of his dress; sky-blue satin cravat, yards of gold chain, with white French gloves, light drab greatcoat lined with velvet of the same colour, invisible inexpressibles, skin-coloured and fitting like a glove.

Number 5 was seldom a dull house, yet during the last twenty years of the Carlyles' occupation, their life was darkly overshadowed. As early as 1846 Jane had begun to doubt whether she still retained her husband's love; and in the 1850's she could not help acknowledging that Mr. C., who had previously appeared indifferent to all women "*as women*," had developed a Platonic infatuation for a famous London hostess, the Junonian Lady Ashburton, and often willingly deserted Cheyne Row to spend his evenings in her company. Meanwhile Jane's health was gradually breaking down, undermined by the enormous doses of henbane and morphia that, as a remedy for her chronic sleeplessness, she had been taking night after night since she reached the age of forty-five. Sometimes she feared she might be going mad, and in 1863 a minor street accident resulted in months of excruciating pain.

It was a disastrous marriage—that is, at least, the conclusion we draw from

The Carlyles relax by the fireplace in their gaily wallpapered front parlor in this 1858 painting by Robert Tait.

the Carlyles' letters. James Anthony Froude, a close friend and the author of a four-volume biography that appeared between 1882 and 1884, asserts that it was never consummated; and certainly Jane exhibited many of the traits of a disappointed and embittered woman whose emotional grievances found vent in a long succession of psychosomatic maladies. Yet was she quite so miserable as she often liked to pretend? Though she would speak of "the Valley of the Shadow of Marriage" and expatiate at length upon her daily woes, both the Carlyles, we must remember, possessed a keen dramatic sense.

For them their checkered married life was an absorbing tragicomedy. Carlyle needed something to grumble about, apart from the current evils of society and the general turpitude of modern mankind; while Jane required a constant supply of subjects on which she could exercise her sharp-edged wit. As a born novelist who had failed to write a book, she may have half enjoyed their misadventures. Her references to her remarkable husband are sometimes tartly disparaging, even downright acrimonious. Yet it is clear not only that she admired him, but that he had aroused

in her a deep devotion, a feeling that soon transcended any youthful dreams of ordinary human happiness.

Both were proud, and both were lonely. During what Carlyle afterward called their "sore life-pilgrimage," they became inseparable fellow travelers. Jane, however, did not cease to fret against his atrabilious egotism—when she was angry, observed a critical acquaintance, she had "a tongue like a cat's, which would take the skin off at a touch"—and her husband was generally far too busy to give her the attention she demanded. Not until he had finally lost her, and had opened her private papers, did he begin to understand her secret sufferings.

Thus the long marriage of Jane and Thomas Carlyle was neither happy nor unhappy. Although its moments of desperate wretchedness probably outnumbered its occasional hours of sunshine, Jane's earliest letters, in which she addresses Carlyle as her "Goody, Goody, dear Goody" and promises him —she is staying at her mother's house— "to make it all up to you in kisses" when she returns to Craigenputtock, are scarcely more affectionate in tone than the last she ever wrote. Written and

posted on April 21, 1866, this letter is headed simply "Dearest."

That afternoon, she drove through Hyde Park, taking a friend's little dog, and when she put it out for a run, it was knocked over by a passing carriage. She dismounted and, finding that it was unhurt, told the coachman to complete their journey. But later he noticed that she was sitting motionless, her hands, "palm uppermost the right hand, reverse way the left," lying quietly upon her lap. She was dead, killed by a heart seizure; and her body was presently carried back to Cheyne Row, to the bed with red hangings she had inherited from her mother and in which she had herself been born. Today, the house that the Carlyles occupied still has a hushed and solemn air, but both its recent custodians have assured me that they have never felt that it was haunted; nor does the smallest spectral influence extend to the adjacent "house of mysteries." I have listened in vain for the sound of Thomas Carlyle's poker thundering against the sitting-room wall.

Peter Quennell, who doesn't keep a parrot or chickens, described Dr. Johnson's Hebridean tour in the Spring, 1973, issue.

A Woman of Courage

Lillian Hellman and I go back a long way. When I was seventeen years old, in the spring of 1956, I played Horace in a high school revival of her play *The Little Foxes* in Barrington, Illinois. I did not realize then, as I do now, that the dramatics teacher who chose to produce that play was taking a mildly heroic political stand.

I was a McCarthyite in the earliest fifties, as much as a fourteen- and fifteen-year-old could be. I believed in the Communist menace, and I thought McCarthy's inquisitorial techniques were as good as those on any radio or television show. I would have been the leading McCarthyite in my class, except that my sometime chum Deke Riley edged me out with a keener sense of dedication to the task, a more highly developed taste for the Jesuitical turn of argument, a more refined killer instinct. I stopped being a McCarthyite less from conviction, or waning conviction, than from having been beaten in schoolboy competition.

I'm glad I did, so that I was able to think myself pure when, during the army-McCarthy hearings and later, I learned of Harry Truman's Loyalty Review Board, of the Attorney General's List, of the House Un-American Activities Committee and Richard Nixon's rise from there to the vice-presidency, of the blacklisting of movie people, of the people like Elia Kazan and Robert Taylor and Clifford Odets who went before the committee and confessed to putative guilt, repented, named others as Communists, helped to destroy the careers of old friends.

I was depressed by this bit of my country's history, but I was not especially moved by it. It seemed lamentable. That was all. And then, some years later, I was astonished—more than as-tonished, physically stunned—to read the letter that Lillian Hellman wrote to the House Un-American Activities Committee in May of 1952 when she was called to testify and expected to name her friends who had, in the past, been members of the Communist party or fellow travelers. She wrote to John S. Wood, the chairman of HUAC:

"I am most willing to answer all questions about myself. I have nothing to hide from your committee and there is nothing in my life of which I am ashamed. I have been advised by counsel that under the Fifth Amendment I have a constitutional privilege to decline to answer any questions about

The House Un-American Activities Committee in 1949 included Richard M. Nixon, second from left, and Chairman John S. Wood, third from left. At right, Lillian Hellman, who testified in 1952.

my political opinions, activities and associations, on the grounds of self-incrimination. I do not wish to claim this privilege. I am ready and willing to testify before the representatives of our government as to my own opinions and my own actions, regardless of any risks or consequences to myself.

"But I am advised by counsel that if I answer the committee's questions about myself, I must also answer questions about other people and that if I refuse to do so, I can be cited for contempt. My counsel tells me that if I answer questions about myself, I will have waived my rights under the Fifth Amendment and could be forced legally to answer questions about others. This is very difficult for a layman to understand. But there is one principle that I do understand: I am not willing, now or in the future, to bring bad trouble to people who, in my past associations with them, were completely innocent of any talk or any action that was disloyal or subversive. I do not like subversion or disloyalty in any form and if I had ever seen any I would have considered it my duty to have reported it to the proper authorities. But to hurt innocent people whom I knew many years ago in order to save myself is, to me, inhuman and indecent and dishonorable. I cannot and will not cut my conscience to fit this year's fashions, even though I long ago came to the conclusion that I was not a political person and could have no comfortable place in any political group.

"I was raised in an old-fashioned American tradition and there were certain homely things that were taught to me: try to tell the truth, not to bear false witness, not to harm my neighbor, to be loyal to my country, and so on. In general, I respected these ideals of Christian honor and did as well with them as I knew how. It is my belief that you will agree with these simple rules of human decency and will not expect me to violate the good American tradition from which they spring. I would, therefore, like to come before you and speak of myself."

She did a hard thing when others were taking the easy way. She risked her career. She risked jail—for a principle—when her friends were taking no risks. Lillian Hellman became a talisman for me.

So I have read her memoirs diligently: *An Unfinished Woman* and *Pentimento*, and—now, *Scoundrel Time* (published recently by Little, Brown). It is in this last volume that she tells the story of HUAC.

She tells it eloquently, with some

By CHARLES L. MEE, JR.

healthy anger and rage—but without rancor or bitterness. The members of HUAC did not disturb her, she writes:

Senators McCarthy and McCarran, Representatives Nixon, Walter, and Wood, all of them, were what they were: men who invented when necessary, maligned even when it wasn't necessary. I do not think they believed much, if anything, of what they said: the time was ripe for a new wave in America, and they seized their political chance to lead it along each day's opportunity, spitballing whatever and with whoever came into view.

She saves her anger for her friends:

I had, up to the late nineteen-forties, believed that the educated, the intellectual, lived by what they claimed to believe: freedom of thought and speech, the right of each man to his own convictions, a more than implied promise, therefore, of aid to those who might be persecuted. But only a very few raised a finger when McCarthy and the boys appeared. Almost all, by what they did or did not do, contributed to McCarthyism, running after a bandwagon which hadn't bothered to stop to pick them up.

One of the ancillary pleasures of history, surely, is to see how the same characters appear and disappear over the course of time, popping up sometimes as good guys and sometimes as bad guys. When Lillian Hellman first received her subpoena from HUAC, she got in touch with that bad guy of the Johnson administration, Abe Fortas, of the law firm of Arnold, Fortas, and Porter. Abe Fortas called on Miss Hellman in New York, listened to her pour out her convictions and feelings of rage and sense of loyalty to former friends. "He admired the china birds on the fireplace, he tried out a few notes on the piano, frowned at the tone, and turned to say that he had a hunch he'd tell me about, but I was not to take a hunch as legal advice. His hunch was that the time had come, the perfect time, for somebody to take a moral position before these disgraceful Congressional committees and not depend on the legalities of the Fifth Amendment." To Fortas the moral position would be to say, in essence, "I will testify about myself, answer all

your questions about my own life, but I will not tell you about anybody else, stranger or friend."

That was, indeed, what Lillian Hellman did, beginning with her eloquent letter. To her great credit and, not so incidentally, to the credit of Abe Fortas, it was dreadful legal advice. As a pure matter of legal strategy, it left Miss Hellman open to the possibility of a jail sentence. As a matter of legal principle, it may be pernicious. She was not, in strict legal terms, allowed to take the protection of the Fifth Amendment for her friends: the Fifth Amendment is precisely for the protection of one's own self, not of one's friends.

Dashiell Hammett, with whom Miss Hellman was living, perceived this fact immediately and warned her that she was heading for a jail term. Yet Lillian Hellman went forth to meet the committee. For her appearance, Miss Hellman had Joseph Rauh as her personal attorney. She volunteered to speak about herself, her past, her beliefs and activities, and she persistently invoked the Fifth Amendment when she was asked to speak about her friends and acquaintances. In the course of her testimony, she referred to the letter she had written to the committee, and the letter was put into the record of the committee's hearings. At that moment Joseph Rauh, to the utter amazement of his client, suddenly leapt from his chair and began handing out mimeographed copies of the letter to the reporters present. Suddenly a loud voice cut through the noises of the hearing room to say: "Thank God somebody finally had the guts to do it."

Until that moment, Miss Hellman had been afraid she could not last until the end of the session. Now the tension was broken. "That unknown voice made the words that helped to save me." The congressmen themselves, sensing the woman with whom they were dealing, questioned her for a mere hour and seven minutes.

Joseph Rauh, who defended other clients before the committee later on, said that Miss Hellman's stand broke the sense of dread that enshrouded the

committee and gave it such remarkable power and so made it easier for those who followed to defy the committee's attempts to go on ferreting out more and more names of alleged subversives. The force of common wisdom commenced to shift over against the committee and against McCarthyism, and so, in simple truth, Lillian Hellman potently helped to halt the panicky witch hunts of the cold war in America, forcefully made history by a courageous statement of principled conviction.

Although Miss Hellman avoided jail by virtue of her action, she was not able to avoid blacklisting, or some half-dozen years of difficulties in getting jobs in her profession. Nor was she herself entirely happy with her appearance before the House Un-American Activities Committee.

I had really wanted to say: . . . "There is no communist menace in this country and you know it. You have made cowards into liars, an ugly business, and you made me write a letter in which I acknowledged your power. I should have gone into your committee room, given my name and address, and walked out." Many people have said they liked what I did, but I don't much, and if I hadn't worried about rats and jail, and such stuff . . . ah, the bravery you tell yourself was possible when it's all over, the bravery of the staircase.

I still think Miss Hellman should have known enough about Stalin's brutality by the late 1930's to have repudiated it; I think she should have done that even though, during World War II, most American politicians were talking about how much alike the Russians and Americans were and how fine a fellow old Uncle Joe was. I like my heroes and heroines to be right all the time—and sooner than the common lot of politicians at least.

And yet, if the function of the artist is to anticipate and imagine various possibilities in life, and to show us what certain courses of action would be if they were acted out, then Lillian Hellman has lived up to her vocation by showing us how to behave with courage when our dignity and liberties are threatened.

The intemperate torch grazed
With fire the umbel of the dark.
The pond-lilies could not stifle
The green descant of frogs.

We had not heeded the warning
That the iron birds creaked.
As we swung the park-gates
Their beaks glinted with dew.

A splash—the silver nymph
Was a foam flake in the night.
But though the careful winds
Visited our trembling flesh
They carried no echo.

Question: Is this poem

 (a) worthless

 (b) a masterpiece

 (c) an elaborate put-on?

Three decades after its composition,
no one is quite sure.
For it is part of a celebrated hoax
that fooled the
critics and set modern poetics askew

How Ern Malley Got the Last Laugh

By ORMONDE DE KAY, JR.

ew satisfactions can match that of watching the experts be made fools of through their own credulousness. Three decades ago, during World War II, ripples of merriment circled the globe with the revelation that Australia's newly discovered bard, Ern Malley, whose posthumously published poems had aroused great interest in literary circles, was not merely dead but had, in fact, never lived, being the fictional creation of two young soldiers with time on their hands.

The creators of Ern Malley had a serious purpose in mind: to demolish the then-current poetic fashion of pretentious obscurantism by holding it up to ridicule. In publishing their handiwork, the two Malley-factors triumphantly made their point. Yet they have been punished, too, in a way they could hardly have foreseen, for their pseudonymous creation has become, in the words of the critic Brian Elliott, "an Australian culture-hero, a figure ten feet tall" who, like some unstoppered genie, not only towers above his creators but threatens to outlast them as well.

The saga began one day early in 1944 in the Adelaide office of the avant-garde magazine *Angry Penguins* (so called from a line of poetry by its twenty-two-year-old founder and chief editor, Max Harris: "Drunks, the angry penguins of the night"). Harris opened an envelope bearing a Sydney postmark and drew from it two typed sheets and a letter written in a round schoolgirl hand over the signature of one Ethel Malley. "When I was going through my brother's things after his death," she wrote, "I found some poetry he had written. . . . It would be a kindness if you would let me know whether you think there is anything in them." Turning to the poems, Harris read the one entitled "Durer: Innsbruck, 1495":

I had often, cowled in the slumberous
 heavy air,
Closed my inanimate lids to find it real,
As I knew it would be, the colourful spires
And painted roofs, the high snows
 glimpsed at the back,
All reversed in the quiet reflecting waters—

Not knowing then that Durer perceived
   it too.
Now I find that once more I have shrunk
To an interloper, robber of dead
   men's dream,
I had read in books that art is not easy
But no one warned that the mind repeats
In its ignorance the vision of others.
   I am still
The black swan of trespass on alien waters.

Harris was impressed. The poem itself was original, the imagery striking, the tone gratifyingly contemporary; and the message, clearly one of high seriousness, declined to yield itself up at once. The second poem, too, turned out to be a magisterial statement clothed in allusive language. Harris dashed off a letter to Miss Malley asking for biographical details and the rest of her brother's poems.

A few days later a fat envelope arrived, containing fourteen more poems under the general title *The Darkening Ecliptic*. In her accompanying letter, Ethel Malley outlined the short and rather bleak life of the late Ernest Lalor Malley—ex-schoolboy, ex-garage mechanic, ex-insurance salesman, ex-watch repairman, loner, and bachelor—who had died tragically the previous winter, aged twenty-five, of Graves' disease. (This ought to have given away the hoax, for Graves' disease is an old-fashioned name for exophthalmic goiter, which is rarely fatal but which renders the victim grotesquely popeyed. "Malley's cow," moreover, is Australian slang for a person who disappears leaving no clue to his whereabouts.) Harris read the poems and showed them to his colleagues, first to a young painter named Sidney Nolan and then to two other editors. Each, as he read, began to share Harris's excitement, for Ern Malley's voice was unmistakably his own, and his vision was powerfully fresh and arresting, as in:

I have been bitter with you, my brother,
Remembering that saying of Lenin when
   the shadow
Was already on his face: "The emotions
   are not skilled workers!"

or in the opening lines of the poem called "Culture as Exhibit":

"Swamps, marshes, borrow-pits and other
Areas of stagnant water serve
As breeding grounds . . ." Now
Have I found you, my Anopheles!

or in such telling similes as:

One moment of daylight let me have
Like a white arm thrust
Out of the dark and self-denying wave

or in this enigmatic assertion, which no one thought to read as a warning:

It is necessary to understand
That a poet may not exist, that his writings
Are the incomplete circle and straight drop
Of a question mark. . . .

Convinced that they were witnessing that rare event, the emergence from obscurity of a truly first-rate talent, the editors warmly endorsed Harris's proposal to print *The Darkening Ecliptic* in its entirety. Harris wrote a foreword in which he hailed Malley as "a poet of tremendous power working through a disciplined and restrained kind of statement into the deepest wells of significance," and when the autumn number of *Angry Penguins* appeared, the first thirty-five pages, about half its contents, were devoted to Ern Malley.

Most of the magazine's nine hundred copies were distributed in Australia, but a few were sent, as usual, to "little magazines" abroad. Ern Malley began to make his name. Harry Roskolenko, an American poet serving in the United States forces in Australia, liked the poems so much that he persuaded a publisher in New York to print several in an anthology. And overseas, word began to filter out from a handful of editorial ivory towers that Australia had at last spawned a major, if unfortunately dead, poet.

Soon, however, Malley's posthumous career was nipped in the bud. At three o'clock one morning in early June, Max Harris was awakened by the ringing of his telephone and informed by a journalist calling from the Sydney *Sun* that Malley's poems had, in fact, been written by two young poets in the Australian army, Lieutenant James McAuley and

Corporal Harold Stewart. Had Harris any comment? Casting about for an answer, Harris muttered, "The myth is sometimes greater than its creators," and hung up. On June 5 the tabloid *Fact* exposed the hoax in print, with a statement by its perpetrators.

They felt, McAuley and Stewart insisted, no "personal malice" toward Harris. They had, however, "observed with distaste the gradual decay of meaning and craftsmanship in poetry," making readers increasingly "insensible of absurdity and incapable of ordinary discrimination." Consequently, they had decided to carry out a "serious literary experiment" to find out whether proponents of modernism—of whom the Angry Penguins were the most conspicuous on the Australian scene—would recognize "deliberately concocted nonsense" when they saw it. In a single free afternoon at Victoria Barracks in Sydney, they had produced the entire lifework of the tragic Ern, and at odd moments in the ensuing days worked out the details of his life.

How the poems were composed made a curious tale in itself. The co-authors had, they said, made use of various books, including the Concise Oxford English Dictionary, a collection of Shakespeare's plays, and a dictionary of quotations.

We opened books at random, choosing a word or a phrase haphazardly. We made lists of these and wove them into nonsensical sentences. We misquoted and made false allusions. We deliberately perpetrated bad verse, and selected awkward rhymes from a Ripman's *Rhyming Dictionary*. The alleged quotation from Lenin . . . "the emotions are not skilled workers" is quite phoney. The first three lines of the poem "Culture as Exhibit" were lifted . . . straight from an American report on the drainage of breeding grounds of mosquitoes.

Australia's newspapers, no less hostile than the hoaxers to surrealism, Dada, and other cultural currents from foreign shores, gleefully embarked on an orgy of derision. Next, American and British wire services picked up the story. *Time* delightedly termed the hoax "as fantastic as a duck-billed platypus," and *Newsweek* declared that McAuley and Stewart had brilliantly proved that "a literary fashion can become so hypnotically powerful that it can suspend the operation of critical intelligence," shaming doubters to silence "by the fear of appearing stupid or (worse crime!) reactionary."

The press, having had its fun, dropped the story. Then a new sensation occurred in the Ern Malley saga: the police brought an action against *Angry Penguins* on the charge that seven of the poems constituted "indecent advertisements" and that certain other items in the same issue were either "indecent, immoral or obscene." (Malley's alleged "indecent advertisements" included such shockers as "The swung torch scatters seeds/In the umbelliferous dark" and "I have remembered the chiaroscuro/Of your naked breasts and loins.")

The trial in September ended in conviction, and Harris was fined five pounds. Outside Australia it went largely unreported, but the shock waves set in motion by the Ern Malley affair continued to shake the underpinnings of faith in some quarters. Thus, in November, the *New Yorker* complained that the McAuley-Stewart caper "spoils anyone for modern poetry for the rest of his life." This proposition failed to be borne out by events. It was further proved wrong with respect to Malley himself, since, fraud though he was, he became the first Australian poet to win a considerable readership outside his homeland.

In the United States, Karl Shapiro and James Dickey acknowledged their debt to him, and critical studies of his work appeared in learned journals. In Britain when *The Penguin Book of Australian Verse* came out in 1958, the absence of his poems was remarked by several reviewers, including the present poet laureate, John Betjeman.

Meanwhile, in Australia, the wounds inflicted on tender sensibilities healed. In 1960 an enterprising producer with the Australian Broadcasting Commission set out to re-create on tape that *cause célèbre* of sixteen years earlier by

interviewing McAuley, Stewart, Harris, and the other participants, including Sidney Nolan, who had since won world acclaim for his paintings. The immediate result was a popular radio documentary that was later broadcast in Britain and the United States. Another result, wholly unforeseen, was that Ern Malley sprang dramatically back to life.

Before long, Malley's *Darkening Ecliptic* appeared as a paperback book with an introduction by Max Harris, excerpts from the radio documentary, and an account of the trial; a blurry photograph on its cover purported to show the author, looking gaunt, unkempt, and appropriately popeyed. The edition quickly sold out. Ten years later the book was reissued, but soon that edition, too, was exhausted. And in 1974 the latest—but surely not last—edition of Ern Malley's poems was published to coincide with the Adelaide Festival of the Arts. This time the cover bore an abstract drawing by Sidney Nolan, Harris and his friends having apparently decided that a gag photograph would no longer do to represent a myth figure of such great, and growing, stature.

For by then Ern Malley was firmly implanted in the Australian consciousness. In art, he is mourned on a monumental scale in a series of large paintings by his early admirer Sidney Nolan. In music, he is memorialized in a jazz suite composed by Dave Dallwitz, one of the original Angry Penguins. And his poetic cycle, *The Darkening Ecliptic*, is a national classic.

How this strikes the two poets who invented Ern Malley and composed his works is anybody's guess. Both men have, over the years, won recognition as poets. Stewart, the author of three books of poems, has been called (by critic Douglas Stewart, no relation) "the only really classical poet Australia has produced"; his predilection for form has drawn him to Japan, where he has made a name for himself as one of the world's foremost translators of haiku. As for McAuley, who has six books of poetry to his credit, he is rated—with A. D.

Hope, his senior by ten years—one of the two giants of Australian poetry. Now nearing sixty, McAuley is professor of English at the University of Tasmania.

McAuley and Stewart can, to be sure, take satisfaction in the knowledge that their victory over the alien menaces of meaninglessness and pretentiousness has proved a remarkably durable one, for Australian poetry remains far more conservative than the poetry of any other English-speaking country. These days even Max Harris writes meticulously crafted verse that makes perfect sense. Still, it can hardly be much fun for the hoaxers to read opinions such as those of Brian Elliott that "neither of them seems ever again to have succeeded in writing with quite the same spectacular abandon which marked the 'Malley' verses," or that "what they had written in the Malley poems was decidedly superior . . . to anything they had written independently." There must surely be moments when they wish they hadn't brought Ern Malley into being that afternoon in Victoria Barracks.

Will the myth, in the end, prove greater than its creators? Lacking authentic heroes in the mold of, say, Washington or Lincoln, Australians have long filled the gap with folk heroes who loom larger than life against the strange outcrops, the weird flora and fauna, and the vast emptiness of their land. Their best-known song, "Waltzing Matilda," celebrates an itinerant workman who falls into a stagnant pool and drowns, while their best-known folk hero, Ned Kelly, is a badman of the outback, who, after his violent death, was swiftly apotheosized into a figure of myth. Given all this—and the Australian sense of humor—it is not difficult to picture, joining the other folk heroes in the national pantheon beneath the Southern Cross, the forlorn and relentlessly urban figure of Ern Malley, who died in his youth, and then attained not just immortality but, better still, the last laugh.

Ormonde de Kay, Jr., is also a poet. He is, however, not at all a fictitious one.

The Olympic Games

Where sport is but a continuation of politics by other means

In the closing days of this, the XX Olympiad, a torch will be lit by the sun's rays at the Temple of Hera in Olympia, Greece. Relay runners will carry it to Athens, and there a Canadian athlete will kindle a flame in the Panathenian Stadium. An ionic sensor will convert the fire into electric impulses that will be transmitted by satellite to Ottawa. A laser beam will reconvert the electric energy into flame, and runners will carry the torch to Montreal for the opening of the XXI Olympic games. For a fortnight thereafter, the youth of many nations will run, jump, ride, swim, lift things, and punch noses while the sacred flame burns in a tall birdbath at the top of Olympic Stadium.

The sensor, satellite, and laser should silence those who say the International Olympic Committee is a self-perpetuating oligarchy of old crocks who do not change with the times. Here they are using the most sophisticated tools of the space age when as recently as 1956 planes and pickup trucks were carrying the torch from Athens to Beirut to Karachi to Calcutta to Singapore to Djakarta to Darwin, whence 2,750 runners lugged it to Melbourne by way of Cairns, Bundaberg, Brisbane, Sydney, Canberra, Wodonga, Bendigo, Ballarat, Geelong, and Footscray. One of them was bitten by a snake.

When the modern Olympics began in 1896, 285 contestants represented ten countries. Four years ago in Munich there were some nine thousand athletes from 123 nations, and unless the trend is reversed the carnival in Montreal will be even larger. To some, this uninterrupted growth proves the health of the Olympic movement. Others see it as a disease like elephantiasis.

Whatever the case, one thing seems clear: the Olympics have grown so big and command such wide attention that they have become an irresistible attraction to any individual or group with a statement to make to the world. Perhaps the festival in Montreal will run its course without untoward incident, but this has not been the case in recent times. No one in the Olympic movement can blot from his memory the events of September 5, 1972, when Arab terrorists invaded the Israeli quarters in Olympic Village and made a blood bath of the Munich games.

Theirs was the most horrifying statement yet made, but it was by no means the first effort to use the Olympics as a forum. The fashion had been set twenty years earlier by a strawberry blonde in a flowing white nightshirt. The opening ceremonies in Helsinki had reached their theatrical peak with Paavo Nurmi, patron saint of Finnish distance runners, carrying the Olympic torch into the stadium, when the Fräulein sprang from the stands, raced around the track to the tribune of honor, mounted the steps, and clutched a microphone.

"*Ystavat*," she said in Finnish, "friends—" and that was as far as she got with a speech in favor of peace. She was only anticipating Henry Kissinger on détente, but a man in gray flannels broke out of a covey of officials, wrapped his arms around her middle, and hauled her, struggling, away from the mike. She was turned over to the cops, who asked her name. "*Sinka*," she said. "I am the sun." Later she gave the more prosaic name of Barbara Rotraut-Player and said she was a student from Stuttgart and represented no organization. "I love God," she explained.

That was 1952. In 1956 Hungarian athletes were just starting for the games when Soviet troops moved into their homeland to crush a revolt. On arrival at Olympic Village in Melbourne they tore down the red, green, and white flag of Hungary's puppet Communist government and ran up the national flag of pre-Soviet days. By the time Russian and Hungarian teams met at water polo, tension had reached the snapping point. Beaten 4–0, the Soviet team came out of the water bleeding and needed a police escort to the dressing room.

Americans remember the flap caused at the 1968 Olympics in Mexico when Tommie Smith and John Carlos lifted gloved fists during the playing of "The Star-Spangled Banner." Carlos and Smith were sprinters at San Jose State and disciples of Harry Edwards, a San Jose instructor who had urged black Americans to boycott the games as a protest against the condition of blacks in the United States. The boycott never came off, but after Smith and Carlos finished first and third in the 200-meter dash they walked to the victory stand and during the anthem stood with heads bowed, not looking at the flag, each lifting a fist gloved in black.

It was a simple, silent gesture lacking neither dignity nor justice, for if the sports arena is where a person is, then that is the place to petition for redress. Among the 80,000 spectators, comparatively few noticed anything amiss, but the Olympic fathers soon made certain the whole world would hear about it. Under pressure from the International Olympic Committee, United States officials banished Smith and Carlos (who had in fact already left Olympic Village on their own to join their wives downtown). Confusing human rights with partisan politics, the waxworks announced, "One of the first principles of the Olympic Games is that politics play no part whatsoever in them. . . . Yesterday United States athletes in a victory ceremony deliberately violated this universally accepted principle by . . . [advertising] their domestic political views. . . . The discourtesy displayed violated the standards of sportsmanship and good manners."

The "universally accepted principle" that the Olympics are above politics is a measure of the IOC's capacity for self-deception. As far back as 1933, when Americans were protesting our participation in the 1936 games in Berlin because of Nazi persecution of Jews, Avery Brundage, then president of the USOC, was saying, "I don't think we have any business to meddle in this question. We are a sports group. . . . When we let politics, racial questions, religious or social disputes creep into our actions, we are in for trouble."

Brigadier General Charles H. Sherrill, an American member of the IOC, talked the Germans into inviting two Jews—Helene Mayer, a fencing champion then living in Los Angeles, and Rudi Ball, a hockey player who had moved to France—to compete for Germany.

"I went to Germany," Sherrill said, "for the purpose of getting at least one Jew on the German Olympic team and I feel that my job is finished. As to obstacles placed in the way of Jewish athletes or any others in trying to reach their Olympic ability, I would have no more business discussing that in Germany than if the Germans attempted to discuss the Negro situation in the American South or the treatment of the Japanese in California."

Said Frederick W. Rubien, secretary of the USOC, "Germans are not discriminating against Jews in their Olympic tryouts. The Jews are eliminated because they are not good enough as athletes. Why, there are not a dozen Jews in the world of Olympic caliber."

It remained for the incomparable Brundage to put it in writing: "Certain Jews must now understand that they cannot use these games as a weapon in their boycott against the Nazis."

No doubt a whole book should be written about Avery Brundage, though if it was faithful to the subject, it would be lamentably dull. Imperious, intransigent, insensitive, incorruptible, and rude, he was a commanding figure in amateur sport in America for more than half a century, and for twenty years he reigned as president of the International Olympic Committee.

He deified Baron Pierre de Coubertin, founder of the modern Olympics, and subscribed without reservation to the baron's view that "the Olympic movement tends to bring together in a radiant union all the qualities which guide mankind to perfection." As the world's foremost guardian of the amateur ideal, Brundage occupied a position comparable to lookout in a prairie dog colony.

A self-described "110 per cent American," he was a member of the America First Committee and he made no secret of his stance on domestic political affairs. "People like me," he said, "haven't had anybody to vote for since Hoover and Coolidge."

This was the man at the top when the IOC opened a can of political worms before the Mexico City games in 1968. The committee voted to readmit South Africa, which had been banned from the 1964 carnival because of the statutory bigotry called apartheid. In the interim the South Africans had promised to send an integrated team to Mexico with whites and nonwhites living together, wearing the same uniform, and marching under one flag.

The fact that South African athletes

would qualify in segregated tryouts and separation by color would remain the rule at home didn't worry the IOC, but forty nations rejected this head-in-the-sand attitude. South Africa's invitation was withdrawn, not because the Olympic brass found its racist policies repugnant, but for fear of a boycott that would embarrass Mexico and jeopardize the future of the games.

Brundage denied that the action had been forced by political pressure. He said it was taken to avoid "ugly violence." Then about two weeks before the Olympics were to open, police and soldiers in Mexico City fired into a student rally in the Plaza of Three Cultures, killing more than thirty people and wounding more than a hundred. Brundage didn't mention ugly violence. He announced: "We have been assured that nothing will interfere with the peaceful entrance of the Olympic flame into the stadium."

In spite of the backstage maneuvering and vote swapping that go on incessantly, and in spite of the double talk that clouds most issues, the Olympic carnival is a magnificent spectacle, an exuberantly colorful pageant. That was true, at least, until the dreadful day in Munich when the fun went out of fun and games.

When the siege in Olympic Village had ended, seventeen persons were dead —eleven Israelis, five Arabs, and one policeman—and three guerrillas were in custody. Yet play had gone on almost without interruption. On the morning of September 5, word came down from Brundage that sport was to proceed as scheduled, and it wasn't until four o'clock that afternoon that a belated sense of decency dictated a halt. Even then, competition already under way was carried to a conclusion. We mustn't give in to terrorism, said the Olympic Committee. We mustn't let a little blood blur the Olympic ideal. A "memorial ceremony" was conducted the next day, but it was more like a pep rally. "The games must go on," Brundage said, and thousands applauded.

At the 1972 games, as in all others, there was also dissatisfaction with the officiating in every sport that is scored by judgment—boxing, wrestling, figure skating, diving, gymnastics. Probably this is inevitable. In the fiercely nationalistic climate of the Olympics, some judges are bound to be influenced by political, ethnic, or religious prejudice. German cries of "*Räuber*" (robber) resounded in the boxing arena when the American light middleweight Reggie Jones was declared loser to Valery Tregubov of the Soviet Union, and complaints were still being heard as the games ended.

The last event was the basketball final between the Soviet and American teams. The United States, which had won sixty-three games with never a defeat in Olympic competition, took a one-point lead in the last half-minute. Taking the ball out of bounds, the Russians moved it to mid-court, where a pass was deflected. Thinking the United States had won the game, the spectators swarmed onto the floor, but the clock showed one second still left to play.

111

The court was cleared, a Soviet player was short with his pass from out of bounds, and time ran out. While the Americans were congratulating themselves, an official ruled that the clock should have shown three seconds left instead of one. On their third chance, the Soviets scored the winning goal. Hank Iba, the American coach, thought they took more than three seconds. (Pushing through the crowd to lodge a protest, he had his pocket picked.)

When it was all over, a spokesman for the Canadian Organizing Committee was asked whether his people were worried about the 1976 Olympics. He said no, they were experienced at dealing with agitators and all would be well in Montreal.

Perhaps it will. Still, I can't help wondering if the modern games may be destined for a fate like the one that overtook their ancient predecessors. The earliest Olympics were religious festivals. The athletes swore to obey the rules, the judges swore to be fair, and the priests sacrificed a pig. A winner was crowned with a wreath of wild olive from a sacred grove near the Temple of Zeus, and he gave public thanks to the gods. While the games were on, all wars among the Greeks were suspended.

Yet as time went on, scandal crept in. The first recorded games took place in 776 B.C., when Coroebus of Elis won a foot race in a meadow beside the river Alpheus in Olympia. In the 98th Olympiad, Eupolus of Thessaly, a boxer, was convicted of bribing three opponents to take dives. He was disgraced, fined, and required to erect a statue bearing his name and offense. In time a long line of these statues, called Zanes, was erected just outside the stadium, paid for with fines collected from cheaters.

When Rome rose to power, it appropriated the Olympics from Greece, but the religious character of the games was lost. Crookedness grew commonplace. In A.D. 66 the emperor Nero swaggered through several events and had himself declared victor in all. Finally, in A.D. 394, Theodosius I abolished the Olympic games. Fifteen centuries passed before they were revived.

De Coubertin believed international rivalry in sports would promote international amity in more important matters.

It is true that the athletes themselves get on well, in the manner of young people everywhere. Yet the intensity of the competition, the temper of the crowds, the prejudices of judges, and the propaganda uses made of the games combine to support a view that the Olympics exacerbate international frictions.

If things get out of hand in Montreal as they did in Munich, there will be a movement to abandon the quadrennial gala in favor of separate world championships in various sports, conducted at separate venues without the hysteria the Olympics can create.

Maybe it isn't necessary to go that far. Perhaps an approach to sanity could be made by eliminating the national flags, anthems, uniforms, and tabulations of medals won and unofficial points scored. If their elders stopped preaching about the honor of representing one's country, the athletes might just go out and play the games for fun.

Red Smith, a sports columnist for the New York Times, *has covered the Olympics since 1948. He won a Pulitzer Prize for sports commentary earlier this year.*